CONTENTS

I dedicate this book to all of the Magdalene girls, and to Helen, Rose, and Bertie who shared this journey with me

I would consider myself to be a 'survivor' after the experiences I went through from the age of sixteen. Being sent to the asylum by mistake, and being falsely accused of a crime, forced me into the role of survivor. I was abandoned by my parents and friends, I soon realized I had no one to turn to, and a life of loneliness was bestowed on me. I quickly had to become emotionally resilient in coping with the vicious treatment bestowed on me by the nuns. I was verbally abused by the nun's, and had to undertake physical labor, and was treated like a slave. The Magdalene asylums were places I had feared my whole life, it was a prison for women, and I was made to feel like a criminal, a feeling that would never disappear.

The Magdalene asylums existed for over seventy years, and they mainly housed unmarried mothers who had children out of wedlock. Women were sent to the asylum for many reasons, such as acting in a promiscuous way, living with a mental illness, or as a result of being a child of a 'fallen woman.'

Every day in the asylum I would have to complete twelve hours of heavy labor, cleaning the linen to purge our sins. We survived our work on just

a small piece of bread and little water. We often finished our work days physically drained and exhausted.

Part of being a survivor was the recovery phase I experienced from being in the asylum. Writing about my experience has been a therapeutic experience and has helped me to consolidate the experiences I have lived through. My story is for the women who suffered during the Magdalene asylums, together we are survivors and our suffering may be over, but our history and experiences will live on forever, and show just how corrupt the Magdalene asylums truly were. For over fifty years I have tried to reform, to move on, and forget about my experiences, but when I look into the mirror and look at my Seventy-five-year-old face, I still see my frightened sixteen-year-old self, looking back at me for a resolution, one I am still fighting for every day.

CHAPTER 1: THE DISCOVERY

In 1955 at the age of fourteen, I lived with my parents, Trudy, a local pharmacist, and My Father Gerald, a secondary school teacher, along with my sister Bertie at our farmhouse in Enniskillen. My mother Trudy was a strict woman, at six feet tall, she had long curly blond hair, and she resembled Doris Day, but her demeanor was sharp and angry. My father was a gentle person, a devout catholic, I would run to him whenever I needed help. My sister, Bertie was sixteen, five foot 10, with perfect long blonde hair, bright blue eyes, and clear Irish skin, the perfect student, and one of the popular girls at our school. I seemed to be the opposite to my sister. I was five foot two, chubby, with wild curly black hair, and only an average student.

I felt I had a very privileged childhood, anything we asked for we got. My room in the attic was perfect. The view from my room overlooked the black horses on our farm and the beautiful mountains in the distance. In our town we were viewed as a respectable family, we were well off financially, and my parents often donated money to the local orphanage and county hospital.

It was at the age of fifteen that my perfect life was about to change forever, and that feeling of peace and serenity was to be nothing but a distant memory.

The morning of my fifteenth birthday was perfect, as I walked down the spiral staircase, the living room was filled with an assortment of balloons with fifteen written on each one. A range of presents was placed on the table wrapped up in white-colored wrapping paper with a red ribbon. As I sat down at the head of the table, I marveled as my parents and Bertie wished me a happy birthday.

An hour later, I made my way to Saint Anthony school, a strict catholic school run by nuns. The nuns in the school made us feel like we were in the army. We always had to be silent in class, our posture had to be perfect, our written work had to be completed with no-fault, we were judged on every move that we made.

I enjoyed the walks with Bertie, she would always make me feel so safe. We would walk up the long narrow country road which led directly to our school.

"How does it feel to be fifteen?"

"No different to being fourteen, I'm still the chubby girl, I feel invisible at school."

"Your young, things will change when you're older," Bertie replied.

"It's easier for you to say, you're seventeen, you'll be leaving for college soon."

"I'll be 70 before I find a boyfriend, by the way how is Michael?"

"Maria, you can't mention Michael to Dad, you have to keep it a secret, I will get fierce hiding from Mum if they find out."

"I won't tell on you, I promise!"

Opposite our school was St Mary's Magdalene asylum, a house for unruly girls. The asylum was protected with steel gates and the building appeared haunted, surrounded by oak trees. When I walked past the asylum, I would sometimes catch a glimpse of one of the girl's walking past the window in their dormitory, dressed in a white gown, their faces pale and full of sorrow.

St Mary's asylum was a place of fear and punishment, we were often warned by the nun's if we were disruptive in class, that we would be sent to the asylum for our sins. Many of the girls sent to the asylums were

treated as the 'outcasts' of our town. The women were sent into the asylum for a range of reasons, including having a child out of wedlock, acting promiscuously, and being born with a mental illness. I was frightened of going to school but the thought of even setting foot in St Mary's would be like entering hell.

As I stood at the gates of the school, Bertie handed me a small present in my hand, a locket, which contained a picture of me when I was an infant and Bertie a toddler. "Put this locket around you, it will protect you from the bullies, and one day when I do go to college, know that I am always here if you need me," Bertie smiled. "Ok," I smiled.

My teacher was a nun called sister Edgar, a wicked woman with long grey curly hair, and she walked slowly with her steel walking stick. Sister Edgar was strict and would give us the Cane if we made a spelling mistake or if we didn't complete our work accurately.

The classroom was cold and damp, the only light we had was through the blinds, there were no photos or pictures on the walls, all that we saw in front of us was the six-foot blackboard.

My best friend would sit next to be in this class Rose Evers. Rose was four foot five, with wild, curly, ginger hair. Rose lived with her father in a townhouse, with her two younger sisters. Ever since her mother passed away, her father became an alcoholic and was repeatedly abusive. Rose lived about a mile from my house. Sometimes at night, Rose would ride her bike to her house and stay over, my mother would prepare the guest room for her, with fresh clothes and towels. Our house was a safe haven for Rose.

Since Rose's mother passed, her behavior worsened as time went by. Rose was very outspoken and angry, and she would often shout out in class, without fear of the repercussions. Today she brought in a homemade birthday card, decorated with red petals. "Happy birthday Maria, everyone it's Maria's birthday!" she shouted.

Suddenly an angry Sister Edgar turned around, her eyes squinted, and her face contorted into anger. "Rose how dare you speak out of turn, how many times do I have to tell you to be quiet in my class!"

"I don't care, can't you calm down for fuck sake!" Rose shouted.

"GET OUT OF my class, let's see how sharp that tongue is at the headmaster's off, go to Mr. Henderson's office Now!" she shouted.

I watched as Rose began to skip out of the classroom, she was so rebellious, so carefree, and I longed to be like her.

Sister Edgar was so full of anger and hate, I would tremble throughout the lesson, worrying in case I answered a question wrong, worried that I would be hit aggressively with her steel cane. As I walked through the corridor that afternoon, I peered into the headteacher's office to find Rose sitting in the isolation room, writing notes given to her by Mr. Henderson.

After school, I peered through the steel gates looking into the Magdalene asylum, as a child I was fascinated to catch a glimpse of the girls inside. We were given the impression that the women in the asylum were unclean, devils of society, criminals, the nuns had brainwashed us all into this way of thinking. As I looked through the gates, I observed the girls sitting in the dining hall, eating a cold unsavory meal at the mercy of the nuns. The girls were distinguished by their dirty white dresses, their cropped short hair, and pale faces.

That afternoon I went home to enjoy my birthday party in our idyllic townhouse, filled with multicolored balloons, party hats, a three-tiered
sponge cake, and my Grandparents Rina and Earl arrived. My Grandmother Rina was extremely strict, and she presented me with my gift, a geometry set, and a notebook. There was no such thing as fun presents. My grandparents believed in being strict towards children at all times, we would have to stand up straight, dress smartly, and not speak when adults were present.

"Maria your dress is filthy, get up the stairs and get changed for Christ's sake!" she scowled.

"Ok Granny," I'm sorry I sighed.

I searched for Bertie that evening. I was confused as to why she was not participating in my birthday celebrations. As I ran upstairs, I could hear Bertie in the bathroom, vomiting. "Bertie are you ok? Ma's going to put the candles on the cake in a minute!" I shouted.

"I'll be down in a second," she yelled.

As I walked past Bertie's room, I could see that the door left halfway open, as I stepped inside, I noticed that her trash can was full, and at the bottom was a pregnancy test. I stood in shock, before running downstairs, hoping I was seeing things. I couldn't tell her what I saw. I

couldn't tell my parents, and I couldn't cope with the reality of the situation. I knew that if Bertie was pregnant that she would be sent to the awful asylum.

That evening I sat in the dining room, as my mother and father, brought out a three-tiered chocolate birthday cake, with two sparklers attached. Rose and Bertie sat in the corner of the room. The only person I could focus on that evening was Bertie. She sat with tears in her eyes, in her oversized brown dress, I knew from her pale, fearful expression that the pregnancy test was positive and that our lives as a family would change forever.

CHAPTER 2: THE PREGNANCY

Time passed slowly after my fifteenth birthday, I found that I was more nervous and apprehensive with each passing day. As time went by, I observed that Bertie rapidly gained weight, and would often wear baggy oversized jackets and jumpers. Bertie was always seen as the girl next door type, her skin was radiant, and she was beautiful, as soon as she entered a room everyone would take notice. I worried every day about her fate. If she carried on and had the baby my parents would send her away without question, and our family name would be destroyed, we would have to face being shunned from the community and church.

Five months after my birthday, I felt it was time to confront Bertie about the pregnancy secret, I could not keep it any longer. It was a beautiful warm sunny day in June, and I walked with Bertie down the long country road to school. We walked through the beautiful daffodil field as the warm breeze from the oak trees brushed past our faces. I watched as Bertie tightened the belt of her large green army coat. "What's wrong Maria you have been quiet all morning it's not like you," she smiled.

"We need to talk, Bertie! I have tried to hide it and ignore what is going on, but I can't take it anymore.

For months you've been hiding out in your room, after school, you've become withdrawn and you wear these ghastly oversized clothes."

Bertie then grabbed me angrily by the arm and dragged me to the bench. "What is wrong with you? This year has been so tough for me, you know how hard I'm working to go to college," she shouted.

"Bertie, I found out the truth on my fifteenth birthday, I found the pregnancy kit, and I know the truth I know your PREGNANT!" I shouted. Suddenly Bertie burst out crying before running away in a fit of hysterics. It was almost a relief to say it out loud, I had held onto my frustration for so long and finally, the truth was out. Seconds later I immediately regretted it.

I sat in Mrs. Edgar's class and we had our general math's exam that we had to complete each year. The exam was taken in complete silence, 'silence' a skill that Rose was unable to master. As we started the exam I

watched as my peers ferociously began to scribble their answers. Whilst Rose began to scribble on the back and draw a picture. I watched as

Sister Edgar sat at her desk, her beady, cold green eyes bore into us as she took a bit into her red apple with her rotten black teeth. Suddenly Rose lifted her exam sheet to show me a colorful drawing of Sister Edgar, with red horns attached to her head, and the words 'psycho bitch' written on the top. I tried to contain my laughter, but I could not hold it in, and I let out a loud screech. It was then that Sister Edgar sprung from her desk like Bambi, "What on earth is going on? I ask for silence in my exam! Right, Rose, go to Mr. Henderson, Maria please see me after the exam."

Seeing Sister Edgar after class was a worse fate than I could have imagined, I spent the rest of the exam dreading my punishment, worried about my fate. As my classmates left the room, I waited nervously in the cold dark classroom, scared and frightened. "Maria, you may come to me now," she growled. I tiptoed towards the desk, as I watched the rage

in Sister Edgar begin to build, her face red with anger, as she held her cane against her chest.
"You ought to count yourself lucky, you are a privileged girl, your parents have good jobs, you come from a happy home, and you have a bright future ahead of you," she scowled.

I began to shiver, in anticipation of the punishment, and in fear that if she knew the truth about Bertie, she would make life harder for me.
"Right Maria, step towards the blackboard and kneel down with

your face forwards on the board." I could feel my whole body begin to shake, and as I knelt, I watched as Sister Edgar raised the stick in the air, and in a stroke of luck the fire bell rang, and we exited the classroom. As I ran along the corridor, I saw Rose standing by the fire alarm, with a devilish look on her face.

"Rose are you crazy? Is this you're doing?" I asked.

"Yeah, Maria, it saved you from a beating from the old bitch so quit gibbering." she laughed.

That afternoon I walked with Rose to her house, a couple of miles from my home next to the village church. Rose's house was so messy, beer

cans littered the floor in the dining room, rats could be seen scurrying around the corners of the rooms. The kitchen sink was filled with a dozen dirty plates and cups, whilst the weeds in the garden towered above the fence. As I walked upstairs, I could see that her father was now passed out on the bed. When I went into Rose's room, it had been left untouched from her mother's passing, the walls were decorated pink, with paintings of moons and imprints of stars on the ceiling. That afternoon we listened to Elvis's first record and danced around the room. When Rose's father woke up, she ushered me to the window for me to make my escape.

That evening, as I walked down the country road, I observed Bertie sitting on a blanket in the cornfield. I walked up to her slowly, "I'm not mad at you Maria, it's nice to know I am not alone. I guess I could never keep a secret from you."

"What are you going to do?" "When will you tell mum and dad?

It was then that a concerned Bertie crawled towards me in desperation. "Mum and Dad must never know; they will send me to the asylum and I'll never be able to leave! You will never see me again!" she scowled

"Will you run away?"

"No, I've worked it all out Mum and Dad are visiting Aunt Helen in Dublin on my due date, when I have the baby, I will give it up for adoption, to Mrs. Cullen."

"Mrs. Cullen the Geography teacher? Are you crazy?"

"No, she is the only other person that knows, and she is happy to take on the child, as she can't have children of her own. Oh, Maria, you are going to have to support me, I can't do this on my own."

"How does Tommy feel about becoming a Dad?"

"Maria, that's enough questions for tonight," Bertie shouted.

It was very hard to watch how weak Bertie had become, she was always so smart, so in control, and I looked up to her, and now she just appeared lost and confused. Even at fifteen years of age, I was fearful of her plan and didn't think it would work out.

A month past and east day I watched as she worked hard to conceal her growing bump. My parents believed that she was in her room studying at night when really, she was sleeping from 7 pm to escape her worries.

Everything changed on April 2nd, at only 6 months into her pregnancy Bertie went into labor during her History examination. I had finished school at 3 pm that afternoon and watched as she was taken into the ambulance on the stretcher. It was so traumatic to watch, her smiling face was contorted to fear and hysterical crying. A crowd of school pupils congregated around the ambulance. "Her waters broke in the exam, who would have thought Bertie Sweeney the goody two-shoes would get pregnant," shouted one girl.

I could feel my heart sink, and I immediately made my way to the hospital which was over two miles away. I ran as fast as I could, I had to be at the hospital quickly before my parents arrived, I feared for Bertie and for
myself. When I arrived at the hospital I looked on in terror as My mother was crouching down on the hospital corridor floor in hysterics. Whilst my

father stood with a vacant expression. "Ma Da, where's Bertie, how is she?" I asked, still my father stood expressionless in his brown suit, with tears filled in his eyes. I burst into Bertie's room and found her in the bed, cowering under the sheet. I looked at her face, she was numb as tears rolled down her face, I placed my hand into hers, and she clenched mine tightly.

"I had a boy Maria, only six pounds, they have taken him away into the neonatal unit. I suppose my parents will put him up for adoption now, I just didn't want this to happen, Maria please go home, I need to speak to Mum and Dad on my own."

It was then that a middle-aged nun called Sister Anita entered the room. Sister Anita had long brown curly hair, her face was pale, and her eyes were piercing blue. I watched as Bertie's face turned to terror, she held the sheets closer to her chest. "I know who you are, you're from St Mary's asylum, why are you here?"
"We have discussed your situation with your parents-"

"No!" Bertie shouted.

"Your parents feel you would benefit from some time at our refuge," she warned.

"No, you can't send me there, my future will be taken away from me. I'll never fit in with those girls," Bertie roared.

Suddenly my parents stormed into the room, my father flew into a rage, "You have given up your rights as soon as you've decided to have a baby, how could you do this to me, to your mother!" he shouted. I watched as his face filled red with anger and rage.

"Maria please go home, this is no place for you," Mum growled. I walked out of the room, grabbed a tray of glasses on the floor, and smashed them on the floor, before running home, and collapsing into a flood of tears in my room. I felt numb, scared, and petrified for Bertie, I hoped that she would convince my parents to take her home so that she could lead a normal life.

CHAPTER 3: THE OUTCASTS

I could not sleep that entire night, I was so worried about the future, and wanted to be with Bertie in the first instance.

I quickly put on my old jogging clothes and ran to St Christopher's hospital, and as I reached Bertie's room, I discovered she was gone, and all that was left was the locket with the picture of me inside, I grabbed the locket and exited the hospital.

As I walked down Smith street, I walked past St Mary's asylum hoping to get a glimpse of Bertie, but it was still only 8 am, I knew I couldn't see her, and I knew my parents would never let me. As I went home, I begged my parents to reveal why they sent Bertie to the asylum, and when she could come home, I was met with ignorance and anger.

That evening as we sat down for our roast Sunday dinner, I watched my mother's vacant face, her eyes were filled with tears, whilst my father sat angrily with his arms folded. Bertie was such a big part of our dinner ritual, she would sing with us, tell us jokes, and impart her medical knowledge she gained from her school studies. I could not take it any longer, I felt like I was going to explode.

"I want to know where Bertie is? I want to see her now!" I yelled. I watched as my father took a big gulp of his milk, before slamming his fists on the table. "Do not ever speak about Bertie again, she has let us down, you will not be seeing her Maria ever again!" He shouted. The veins nearly burst in his face. I watched as my mother ran out of the kitchen in hysterics and despair.

The result of Bertie having a baby caused a devastating impact on us as a family, we had gone from the most respected families in the town to the outcasts of the town. My mother was turned away from our local church from Fr Richard, my father became embarrassed sitting in the local pup when all the people around were whispering about him, he became a recluse.

At school Sister Edgar, would call me disrespectful names and would scowl at me for the slightest mistake in my work. In the afternoons when I returned home from school I would observe my parents rowing in the kitchen, throwing plates at each other, blaming each other over Bertie's mistake. I would hide upstairs in my room and listen to my Elvis record and escape the world.

I would think about Bertie all the time, I wondered where she was and if she was safe. In our classroom, we had a view of the gardens of St Mary's asylum. I would try to sneak a glance at the girls walking around in the garden, but still, there was no sign of Bertie.

Each afternoon, after school I would sit on the bench overlooking the Magdalene gardens. Sometimes Rose would sit next to me, but her attendance was so poor, I never did have the time to enjoy her company. Rose would sing her favorite song from calamity jane, and eventually, try to coax me into singing. I always admired her strength and courage despite her awful home life with her father.
I would sit on the bench after school feeling so low and depressed. I was ignored by my fellow peers at school, and I could feel all my classmates laughing and sniggering behind my back, I wanted to escape this awful life forever.

Weeks passed by and a month after her disappearance I witnessed Bertie in the garden, and we locked eyes. I looked on in despair. She was now extremely skinny, dressed in her dirty white garment, her face

was pale with dark black circles, and her hair was cropped short, stripping her of her femininity. I could feel my eyes fill up with tears as she walked towards me.

"Oh Maria, it's cold, what are you doing sitting out here? It's great to see you"
"I've waited so long to see you, Mum and dad never told me what happened at the hospital."

"Well, we can't change what happened, Maria,"

"What have they done to you? Your skinny as a rake, you have bruises on your arms, for fuck sake Maria you look like a boy!"

"Please don't swear! It is ok in here really, yes it can be tough, but I will get through.

"This is not ok, I may be fifteen, but I know what's going on, Bertie. I have to get you out of that place or you will never leave!" I shouted.

I watched as Bertie started to panic as she nervously looked around to see who was watching. "Look I have to go now but meet me here at this time next week, Maria."

I walked towards the gate and passed the locket she gave to me into her hands. I watched as she put the locket nervously into her pocket. As she walked off into the distance, I felt a tear run down my cheek. I was so sad but realized I had to stay strong, I was on a mission to save Bertie.

CHAPTER 4: THE CRIME

Time seemed to pass by so slowly without Bertie each week I would go to see her, and I would talk about school and Bertie would help me with my homework, we made a rule not to talk about my parents or home life. I still felt like the invisible girl at home, and nothing I said or did seemed to matter.

Two years after Bertie left us and home life felt like a prison, I was sixteen now, and my parents monitored every movement I made, fearful I would make the same mistake as Bertie. The only joy I gained from life was spending time with Rose and seeing Bertie after school. As each day passed, Bertie would appear weaker, the Nun's would not allow her to grow her hair, her knees and arms were covered in bruises, and she was skinny as a rake following her hunger strike.

My final visit to Bertie was very traumatic, I did not realize how much I needed her. It was later after 4 pm and I was talking to Bertie about school and my sixteenth birthday party. It was then that I observed an angry nun, with long grey curly hair, come charging towards Bertie, she grabbed her angrily by the arm.

"What on earth do you think you are doing? You are not allowed to speak to people outside of this house!" she yelled. "Come to my office now!" she screamed.
It was then that I tearfully watched as Bertie walked off into the distance. I knew the nuns would monitor her closely, and that I would never see her again.

My parents treated me like a slave as soon as I came home from school, I was made to clean the house and scrub the floors, and for the rest of the evening, I was instructed to study for my final exams. Even two years after Bertie left us, we were still unable to move in and we were segregated from others in the town.
On November 5th, 1958 my fate was about change forever. It was a cold, dark, and gloomy evening. The rain crashed against the windowsill, as I completed my math homework, and the thunder and lightning continued through the evening. Then at 7 pm I heard a knock on the window, I looked on in disbelief, at a drenched Rose crouched down on the window ledge, her grey overcoat was soaked through, and her Red curly hair seemed extra frizzy. Rose opened my window and jumped onto the floor.

"Rose what are you doing here? You know Ma doesn't want you at the house!" I pleaded

"Maria I can't take it anymore, Da has just thrown the bottle of whiskey at my face, he could have killed me," she cried. I could see the deep bruising on Rose's forehead.

"Look I'd love you to stay here but-"

Suddenly Rose grabbed me by the hand, "c'mon we're going out there's something we need to do!" Rose ushered me towards the window.
"We can't go outside what if we get struck by lightning?"
"Don't be stupid you silly bitch!"
We jumped outside and we ran down the long country path until we reached the school nun's house, which housed Sister Edgar and three other wicked nuns. We stood behind the bush which led to the pebble path towards the cottage house.

"Why are we here, Rose, what's going on?"

"We are going to burn down the house!"

"Rose that is murder!"

"No, the nuns are at Mass, at St Thomas, it's fine," Rose whispered.

I watched in terror as Rose ran down the path, dropping a scarf through the letterbox, before pouring petrol inside and lighting a match. Rose stood at the doorstep, "All done!" she shouted.
It was then that I observed Sister Edgar watching us from the up-stairs window, I ducked down behind the bush, hoping that she did not see me. I ran down the path, and Rose joined me.

"We have to run. Rose, Sister Edgar was in the window looking out if she saw you or me, then that's its game over!" I shouted. I could feel my heart pounding against my chest, as I ran with fear and terror. I worried now that Rose's behavior would be the final straw and seal our fate.

In the distance, we could hear the police car's coming from behind us, until they stopped suddenly, and a policeman exited the car, arresting

both me and Rose for arson. I watched as Rose attempted to wrestle the policeman, but I stepped into the police car in a calm manner. I was petrified and began to tremble as we continued down the country road. I believed if I stuck to my story, that they would see that Rose caused the fire. I was innocent. I knew I would have to plead for my innocence.

I spent over two hours in the cold white-walled police station, with a middle-aged long-bearded policeman, constantly questioning me looking at me in contempt. I pleaded my innocence foolishly saying I was not at the scene, and met Rose along the road, not wanting to give too much away. I didn't realize the worst was yet to come, Sister Edgar arrived in her red cloak, and stood behind the glass, I could feel her Icey gaze bore into me, she was seething with anger and rage. Then My parents arrived, my father's face was red with rage. Then they all disappeared leaving me alone in the room.

I began to walk around in circles in the room, I convinced myself they would find Rose guilty of arson, and they would be sent home with just verbal warning.

Rose had a bad history and reputation in the town, breaking into local shops and into the houses of our neighbors. I had to wait for an hour before my parents walked into the room, my mother was hysterical while my father was trembling with tears filling his eyes.

"How could you do this to us? After everything that has happened to us as a family another daughter has let us down, our daughter a killer!" he shouted.

"Da I didn't do anything, it was Rose, I didn't start the fire!" I pleaded.
It was then that the aggressive policeman ushered me to sit down. "We have a written confession from Sister Edgar, she witnessed you going to the letterbox of her house and she witnessed you pouring petrol through the letterbox."

I could feel my heart sink and I collapsed onto the floor in shock, "I didn't do anything, she's lying, Ma and Da she is wicked! I would never do this. You have to believe me, can we just go home please?" I asked.
It was then that my mother crept up from the floor and regained her composure, before looking at me in contempt.

"No, you won't be coming home, you can't Maria, we can't have a criminal living at our house." she cried.

"No Ma what are you saying? No one is listening to me, let me explain. Please!" I shouted.

Suddenly two guards walked in, the same guards who escorted Bertie from the hospital into St Mary's house. I held onto the legs of the table with all of my might.
"I'm not going to that awful place, you can't send me there, I won't be imprisoned like Bertie!" I shouted. I held on angrily onto the table, but the guards viciously grabbed my hands pulling me away, carrying me out. I glanced at my parents as they looked on with no emotion, no feeling, no compassion. The guards dragged me outside into their black Cadillac, as the rain poured down. I was terrified as I sat in the back seat, I knew my life was about to change forever. In the car, I was so angry with Sister Edgar for falsely accusing me of starting the fire.

CHAPTER 5: THE MAGDALENE GIRLS

After an hour in the car, we finally arrived at St Mary's home. The two guards escorted me in. I looked up at the grand, tall, creepy, three story mansion. I was hoping to see Bertie, and she could help me out of this terrible situation. As we entered the steel doors was led down a cold gloomy corridor, it felt like an eerie boarding school, with rusty blue painted doors, a dining room

with hundreds of tables and chairs, and I was immediately led to the Sister Rita's office, the head of St Mary's asylum.
Sister Rita had long brown hair, her face was tanned and wrinkled, she constantly frowned, as she looked at me as if I was an insect.
The office was cold and damp, with a bookshelf filled with religious books, and files of the girls in the asylum.

"Sister Rita please let me go home, this has all been a terrible misunderstanding, I didn't start to the fire just let me explain." I pleaded.

"Oh you do not need to explain to me Maria, I have had a phone call from Sister Edgar explaining everything, she saw you do it, yes you were pushed into it by your friend Rose, but you initiated the attack," she smirked.

"That is not true, it's a pack of lies!" I shouted.
Suddenly Sister Rita grabbed me by the arm, her breath smelt like whiskey, her evil green eyes soared into mine.
"You are here for the foreseeable future, and you are here to repent, just like Mary Magdalene, you will repent for your sins.

I started to cry in frustration, knowing that Sister Rita was not going to listen to me, I was terrified at the thought of being confined to the asylum, this was my worst fear. I believed one day that I would have saved Bertie and she would escape to another country to live her life again.

"At least can I request to stay with my sister Bertie, I don't want to be alone here, and I know she will support me. Where is Bertie? Can I see her now?" I asked.

"Never mind Bertie, I will have Sister Margaret show you to your dormitory now."
I immediately felt concerned about how Sister Rita disregarded Bertie so quickly. I wondered if she was safe. Why were they keep-

ing Bertie away from me? Has she finally escaped? I had never felt so nervous, I was

sick with nerves. Sister Margaret walked in a young Nun in her late twenties, she had long blonde hair, pale skin, and the startling blue eyes.

"Hello, you must be Maria, I've come to take you to your dormitory on the third floor." she snooped. Sister Margaret's manner was cold and sharp and angry in her demeanor. I followed her up the rusty old spiral staircase, I could hear girl's giggling in their rooms. Sister Margaret walked me outside of a room at the end of the corridor. "Maria this will be your new room, your clothes and nightdress are on your bed, breakfast is at 7 am and chores start at 7:30 am."

"Wait, I need to speak to my parents, please," I begged, but Sister Margaret walked off into the distance.

I nervously walked into the room and observed six girls, sitting on their old wooden beds, looking at me in awe and silence. The girls were a mix of ages from fourteen to twenty-one. I walked towards my bed which had a single grey sheet, and an old white creased dress, that I would wear for the night, and black paper nightclothes.
It was then that the girls individually introduced themselves to me.

The first girl was fifteen-year-old Kaitlyn. Kaitlyn was five-foot-tall, pale with short black hair and desperately thin. Katelyn was sent to the asylum, for assaulting her stepmother by firstly striking her with an iron and then pushing her down the stairs. Kaitlyn explained that she pushed her stepmother in self-defense after years of abuse. Katelyn was rebellious and a free spirit.

Next to Kaitlyn in the next bed was Dawn, Dawn was twenty-one, six-foot, and was the oldest girl in the dormitory. Dawn was sent to the asylum at the age of sixteen, after becoming pregnant by her older college boyfriend. Dawn was like the mother of the group, supporting and caring for all the other girls in the room.

Adjacent Dawn was Helen, Helen was shy and withdrawn, she was very thin, with messy cropped brown hair. Helen was diagnosed with schizophrenia later in life, but was sent to the asylum for 'troublesome' behaviour, and at eighteen she was a difficult pupil at my school. The nun's and teachers at the school could not control her difficult behaviour and they saw no alternative but to send her to the asylum.

Next to Helen was Eileen, Eileen was seventeen and had a razor-sharp tongue, she was visibly angry and defiant against the nuns in the asylum. In appearance Eileen was short and chubby, she had beautiful clear skin, with brown eyes and wild long curly brown hair. Eileen was sent to the asylum following the promiscuous behaviour she displayed in her all girl's catholic high school, including getting caught smoking and drinking by the nun's office and breaking all the rules.

Then there was Jane, Jane was fifteen and had a bright and vibrant personality, at five foot three and short blond hair, she had been in the asylum her entire life and was an orphan to an unmarried mother. Jane's innocence and carefree nature was infectious, she was the only person in the dormitory who was settled, she had never known a life other than that in the asylum.

"Well there is no way I can stay in this rotten room, the floor is damp, the bedsheet is dirty. I won't cope!" I shouted.

"You will find your way, eventually, if you need anything Maria you come to me, I will help you!" Dawn smiled.

"Help? She doesn't need help. That girl was born with a silver spoon, she'll never make it through, she will crumble!" Eileen snapped.

Suddenly we had a loud thud at the door, "keep it down in there!" shouted the voice of one of the guards."

I watched as the girls slipped under their covers fearful of the authoritative tone of voice of the guard.
I crept slowly towards the window, overlooking the magnificent grounds, the ten-acre garden, the mountains in the distance, the beautiful scenic village down. As I looked up to the sky, I could see the full moon, which lit up the field, and cast a shadow over my face. I had spent over two years gazing into the gates of the asylum, speaking to Bertie, imagining the terror she was being subjected to. I felt I was trapped and locked in my own snow globe, hidden from the outside world, defiant I was not going to be another statistic in the asylum. I walked towards my bed and threw

the dirty nightdress on the floor, and shivered in the cold room, and began to cry myself to sleep.

CHAPTER 6: THE SLAVE IN THE LAUNDRY

The next day I woke up to a thundering horn being rung from outside of the room, "Get up girls," roared sister Rita.

We quickly got dressed, and I soon felt like a homeless person, in the white shroud. I was thankful to Dawn for supporting me in the morning, "Just follow me today, keep quiet, avoid eye contact with the nun's if possible, remember as you know they will be watching you," she warned. As we all got dressed for the day, we made our way out of the room in single file, we were soon joined by the other two hundred girls from the other dormitories. The girls were all compliant and walked with a look of fear on their faces as if they were criminals.

We walked in silence into the dining room, and sat at the brown rotten wooden tables. Sister Rita and sister Margaret stood at the front of the dining room with bibles in their hands, whilst a young girl Esmeralda stood reciting the 'our father' prayer whilst we followed her in unison. As I said the prayer, I frantically gazed around the room looking for Bertie, desperate to find her, desperate to bring comfort to this awful situation.
It was then that the cook moved frantically around the room with her trolley, with five tubs of cold stale porridge. She scooped the porridge into

my bowl and in shock of the awful taste I spat it out, "This is cold!" I stammered, not realizing that my voice echoed throughout the room. I observed the girls in my dormitory crossing their heads in disapproval. Then Sister Rita charged towards me angrily. "You must never talk at mealtimes or in the laundry rooms, it is the height of disrespect, do you understand?" she screamed. I watched as her face turned boiling red with anger, the vessels in her head looked fit to burst. I could not comprehend why she was so angry over something so trivial.

After breakfast, we continued into the laundry room, and sister Margaret took me to one side to explain the working rules in the laundry. I looked on in terror in the laundry room, there were over fifty large washing basins with dirty sheets stacked up against each one, some of the basins had a step stool for some of the shorter girls. In the bowls was hot water mixed with starch.

The view from the room was of the church courtyard, a place where the nuns would sit outside and mock us in full view.

"Well Maria this is the laundry room, you will spend most of your day here from 8 am to 6 pm with half an hour lunch break at 12. Your job is to clean the linen in the bowl and fold it and leave it to dry.

There is to be no talking in here unless instructed by the nuns. Some days you will be instructed to scrub the floors of the corridor," Margaret stammered.

I nervously made my way over to the basin, next to Dawn, hoping she would help me, "why do we have to do this?" I asked.
"The nun believes that by doing this we are purging our sins, stop talking, you don't want to get caught," she whispered.

I grabbed the linen and threw it into the basin and began to scrub the dirt off the sheet, after a few hours my knuckles became sore and my hands ached. My back started to ache as I bent over the hot basin, I looked at Dawn's hands as she cleaned the linen, her hands were raw red and cracked. I wondered how long I would have to do this, it didn't feel like it work it felt like torture.

Halfway through work, I could hear a familiar voice giggling in the corner of the room, it was Rose. I could see her standing by the fire exit as she completed her laundry. I slowly put the linen on the floor and crept towards Rose, her laughter quickly turned to shock as she looked up at

me. I could feel a surge of anger rush through me and I charged towards Rose pushing her to the ground and I began to hit out. "This is all your fault, it was you that set the fire! You have ruined my life!" I screamed.
Rose began to cover her face to protect herself, before Sister Margaret and Sister Rita broke up the fight and I was ordered to Sister Rita's office.

"You are in the wrong place if you think you can break the rules at St Mary's house. First you speak out, now you caused a fight. You will learn the hard way until you follow the rules, she shouted. Kneel down now!" She commanded.

"I've been trying to tell you Sister please; I didn't start the fire you have to believe me!" I pleaded.

It was no use as I knelt, Sister Rita grabbed a cane from under the desk and hit me across the back fifteen times, each hit scalded me, each hit made me fiercely determined I would fight for justice.

After the punishment, I felt so weak and ran upstairs and collapsed onto the bed in desperation.

The girls entered the dormitory and saw how upset I was, "look at you, you can't even last a day here, you have made an enemy of sister Rita already." Eileen barked.

"Shut up Eileen, you remember how hard it is when you're new, you just have to play the rules, if you do as they say you won't be punished." Dawn smiled.

"Do as they say and or risk staying here for the rest of my life. Does anyone actually escape this place?"

"Well there are two ways people leave here, they either escape or are collected by a family member after an extended period of time." Eileen smiled.

"I wanted to ask, has anyone seen a girl called Bertie here? She's about eighteen, she's my sister, she was sent here for two years?" I asked. The girls in the dormitory shook their heads unaware of who she was.

I watched at 9 pm as the girls were asleep in bed, exhausted after working all day. A part of me wanted to smash the windows and attempt

to escape, I wanted to scream, and plead for my innocence, whatever the cost.

At 11 pm that night I could hear Helen crying in the bathroom. I tiptoed into the bathroom to see how I could help her. "What's wrong Helen?" I observed her trying to wash, she appeared confused and muddled. "Maria, can you help me please to watch my back?" she asked.

I agreed to help her and looked on in terror as she lifted her top up, I could see several deep scars on her back from the punishments given by the nuns, over her long period of stay. I gently wiped her back with the sponge, I knew I was in some form of unimaginable hell, and I could not imagine being imprisoned in St Mary's for life.

CHAPTER 7: THE REVELATION

My second day was filled with a small amount of hope and optimism. As I spent the morning working in the laundry, I noticed another girl trying to get my attention, I was too scared to respond, too scared about the consequences. At Lunchtime as I went to the dining hall to have the cold and stale soup, that was left to swing for over an hour. The girl who tried to get my attention was Stacey Smith. "Hi, are you Maria? I have something of interest for you to see in my dormitory, but you must be quick," she warned. I hurried along the staircase to the third floor and Stacey took me into her room, a single room with her bed and another vacant bed by the window.

"Your Bertie's sister, right? I recognize you from the picture?"

"What picture?" I asked.

Stacey moved towards the vacant bed and lifted the mattress and pulled out various watercolor paintings, including a self-portrait of myself, a black and white drawing of our family cottage home, and a diary which included drawings with several diary extracts.

"You see, me and Bertie were sent to this room to isolate from the other girls, as punishment, we didn't follow the rules and we tried to escape multiple times. She talked about you all the time, she was so proud of

you, she thought you were stronger than she ever was," Stacey explained.

"What happened to her? Did she finally escape?" I asked

"It was the strangest thing, I woke up one day and she was gone, I tried to ascertain from Sister Rita about what happened to her, but she ignored me,"

"What did she do here apart from draw, did she find some form of contentment?" I asked.

"Bertie really wanted to leave, she wanted to train for her medical degree, and she was determined to lead a happy life,"

I walked over to the vacant bed and the bed was still unmade from when she last slept in it. I lifted the pillow and I could still smell the fragrance of her hair and the smell of her beetroot perfume. On the wall beside her bed, she had carved her name under the window ledge.

I thanked Stacey and we made our way downstairs and back to the laundry room to complete our evening duties. The nun supervising Sister Helena, was a former Magdalene girl who was sent to the asylum when she was fifteen, and never left. She was six-foot five, strong build, chubby, with a wicked-looking face and hair was tied up in a bun, she gave the appearance of Mrs. Trunchable from Matilda. I wondered how she could be so brainwashed into thinking that being a nun was a good option. Later that evening she ordered us all into the dining room for a 'treat'

"Right girls, it's time for our monthly inspection, you are all to remove your clothes," Sister Rita laughed, standing beside Margaret and Helena. I watched as the girls began to awkwardly undress and I felt compelled to join them. It was then that Sister Margaret and the other nun's burst out in hysterics making degrading remarks about features of our body. "Look at you Maria you have a very tiny bottom, turn around so we can see it!" She smiled. I looked at the other girls around me, some were in tears, others were red with embarrassment, mortified at how cruel the nun's actions were.

I watched the tension and anger build up in Eileen, she stood with her hands clenched. "Why don't you strip for us sisters let us see your old saggy disgusting bodies, let's see who's laughing then!" Eileen shouted, before running out of the room, whilst Margaret and Helena chased her with a Cain.
"Quickly girl's put your clothes on," Sister Margaret chastised, with no remorse shown on her face. Following her outburst Eileen was sent to the isolation room on her own, for a week, to repent for her sins.

That afternoon the nun's granted us a half an hour break in the courtyard outside. Standing by the gate was Sara Armstrong, an old friend I had at school, she was ushering me over to speak to her. I had known Sara since I was four years old. Sara was five foot three with short blonde hair, emerald eyes, and glowing skin, she stood in her red coat excited to see me. I was so nervous seeing her, fearing judgment, and any distasteful words used against me.

"Hello Maria, it's great to see you, I just want to offer my support to you, I was so shocked to see that you were sent here,"

"Look, Sara, if you have come to gloat, I really have not got the patience," I commanded.

"No Maria, I'm really here to offer you a friendly ear, I knew when I heard that you set fire to the house that you didn't do it, I knew it was something Rose would do. Really Maria, I just want you to know that when you leave this place, you're welcome to see me anytime." she smiled.

"Just go Sara, I'm not interested in your pity, you just want to show to your friends that you've spoken to the town outcast, you repulse me!" I shouted, before running away. I was so harsh on Sara, but I felt like I could not trust anyone, I felt judged and villainized ever since Bertie was sent to the asylum, and my entrance made me feel like the ultimate outcast. The nuns would strip us of our dignity, we felt unclean and inferior to people on the outside.

CHAPTER 8: THE MAGDALENE STORIES

My first week in the asylum was the most physically and mentally draining experience I was yet to experience. I was not used to working all day long and being treated like a slave. All the rumors before I entered the asylum about the treatment of the girls appeared to be true, we were not treated as humans we were treated like depraved criminals who needed to be punished.

On Friday we were all delighted to hear that our work duties were to be suspended, due to an infestation of rats in the workroom, Eileen joked about the rat's attacking the nun's and eventually killing them!

The time together in our rooms allowed me to get to know the girls and their pasts better. We all shared stories about how we entered the asylum and our lives before.

Katelynn explained that she lived in a small cottage with her father, an engineer, and her mother who was a nurse. Katelynn's Mum passed away when she was fourteen and after she passed her father met and quickly married a Twenty-five-year-old lady called Sally, who Katelynn believed was as evil as a witch. Sally completely transformed the beautiful cottage into a barbie dream house, all the walls were painted

pink, and eventually, all the photos of her mother slowly disappeared. Sally was breathtakingly beautiful, six-foot-tall, slim, with bright sea blue eyes. Katelynn explained that Sally played the dutiful wife for a year, before her behaviour drastically changed after a year. Katelynn explained she would do things to encourage her father to turn against her. Sally would hide her father's work documents in her room, break furniture and blame Katelynn, and in her evilness, she would hurt herself to create bruises on her body and blame Katelynn as the culprit.

Despite her actions, Kaitlyn's father still held onto the close relationship he had with her. One day Katelynn realized how evil Sally was when she took it into her hands to try and kill her once and for all. One afternoon When Katelynn was cleaning the kitchen floor, Sally viciously knelt and wrapped the cord of the iron around her neck and began to squeeze it tightly. She pulled desperately on the cord, as she could feel herself go in and out of consciousness. Then in a fit of rage Katelyn punched out at Sally knocking her onto the floor whilst hitting her with the iron in an angry outburst. The vicious attack left a scalding bruise on Sally's face which made her resentful, and her father became wary of Katelyn's behavior.

On Christmas Eve everything came to a terrible climax. Katelynn was due at the local church for her piano performance at the school hall in front of a prestigious high-class crowd. Her father bought her an expensive red ball gown to wear, whilst Sally grew more and more jealous at not being the center of attention, Just before they were about to leave Katelynn stood at the top of the stairs calling out for her father to hurry to avoid arriving late. It was then that disaster struck, as Sally swung open the door and came charging down the hallway towards Sally in her black witches' cloak, with her fists clenched, and her face full of anger. Sally quickly realized that she was about to attack, and she ducked causing Sally to fall down the stairs.

Katelynn observed Sally laying in a pool of blood at the bottom of the stairs, she was dead.
Kaitlyn's father immediately believed she was the culprit, and after a long engagement at the local police station, he was encouraged to send her to the asylum.

Dawn then explained her traumatic story about her arrival at the asylum at fifteen years of age. At fifteen, Dawn became involved with a seventeen-year-old college boy, and after a few months of dating, she became pregnant. Dawn's mother and father initially supported her during the pregnancy but adjusted the size of her clothes to conceal the baby bump. Her parents led her into a false sense of security that they would support her in the future. Then in a cruel twist of fate when the baby finally arrived, Dawn's mother called for the guards of St Mary's to escort her from the hospital to the asylum, in order to hide the shame of what happened and to conceal the truth forever.

As an exhausted Helen slept Dawn offered insight into her troubled life. Helen's parents were very poor and worked in the coal mines, they worked long hours and as soon as they arrived home they would spend hours drinking whiskey, leading to troublesome physical outbursts and violent rage. In order to protect herself from her parent's behaviour, Helen would hide out in her room in the loft, clutching her teddy bears,

shaking in fear and often crying to sleep. It was Helen's depression that worsened her physical state.

Eileen explained that she came from a privileged background, her mother and father were both doctors, and she had everything she wanted in her townhouse. Eileen's behavior however was out of control, during lessons at school she would frequently call out, swear at the nun's, and lie about her character claiming she was having sexual relations with the boys in the private school just to anger the religious elders.

The Nun's in the catholic school saw Eileen as a 'problem' and as an insect that needed to be squashed. Eileen's behaviour had reached breaking point when a bully at school had ripped up her artwork; she was due to submit for her finals. In retaliation she viciously cut her hair, cutting into her scalp, and then proceeded to punch and kick her on the floor. Sister Rita convinced Eileen's parents that she required 'correction' at the Magdalene asylum.

The break that we had from working in the laundry was much

needed, we needed to relax our worn-out bodies, and we were all thrilled when the laundry room was closed for an extra day. We spent the day talking about our life together, at night Dawn would tell us the wildest ghost stories which helped us to escape the nightmare we were going through.

CHAPTER 9: ESCAPE

Months had passed in the asylum, and I soon realized the import-
ance of being resilient to the nun's actions. I felt almost immune
to the nun's wicked behavior and realized that aggression, humiliation, and constant ridicule was part of the experience. I decided to follow the rule book, I worked hard in the laundry, kept
quiet when I was supposed to, and avoided confrontation at all
times. I attempted to butter up the nun's in a failed attempt to be
treated with mutual respect.

One day in September 1958, everything was about change and I was about to feel the full wrath of Sister Rita.

It was a cold freezing morning and it continued to snow, and outside we could see thick blankets of snow covering the mountains over a misty fog.

Dynamics had changed in the laundry room, we could take three twenty-minute breaks, which allowed us to refresh and prevented us from collapsing into exhaustion. Rose now had grown a close connection to the girls in the laundry, including Eileen as they were both

similar and fiery characters. As I completed the laundry that morning I watched as Eileen snuck her dirty laundry into Rose's pile to offload work

onto her. As soon as Rose noticed Eileen's trick, she charged towards the large basin pushing it over pouring the hot water all over the floor. Both girls entered a vicious fight swearing at each other and hitting out. All the girls were sent out of the room, whilst the floors were left to dry.

As I walked along the corridor, I noticed a familiar voice, a familiar scream from Sister Rita's office, as I looked through the keyhole I looked on in terror. The girl in the room being attacked was Helen, she was kneeling in front of Sister Rita whilst the local Priest, Father Michael, proceeded to beat her across the back with the cane. How could he do this, a man who has taken his vows at the catholic church? How can a 'respected' man act in this way? I ran out of the room in terror and went outside into the courtyard and collapsed in tears into the snow. Helen was so innocent, she was mentally ill, and the staff never took the time to understand her. Helen could not help her behaviour, but the nun refused to offer the care and support she needed, and she was villainized.

As I gathered my thoughts in the snow, I heard shuffling at the gates. As I looked at the gate, I could see the shadow of a girl in a white dress leaving the asylum. It was then that a surge of adren-

aline rushed through
me and I trudged through the snow and opened the gate and I was free. Just like that, I was free. The gate was never unlocked before, as girls would usually escape from climbing over the walls. As I looked around outside, I could not see the mysterious girl. I quickly ran through the snow and found a shallow hole behind an oak tree as I could hear the bell ring. Every time a girl had escaped the guards would ring the bell, little did I know that I had left my headband by the door,

I was petrified as I lay in the dugout until I felt a hand on my shoulder, it was Dawn, in her white dress carrying a satchel. "What are you doing you silly bitch?"
"I saw the door open and followed you, how did you open the gate?"
I could see how frantic Dawn was as her hands trembled in my shoulder, "Right take off your shoes, we need to run, you need to keep going and run as fast as you can." she warned.

It was then that Dawn held onto my hand and we ran with all our might through the deep snow, my home was less than a mile away and as we reached the village, I watched as Dawn climbed into a delivery van.

"Look, Maria, just go home, we can't hide out together it is too risky,"
"They won't accept me. I will be sent back," I pleaded.
It was then that Dawn slammed the doors shut off the van filled with potatoes. I felt defeated, but quickly realized that this was Dawn's escape, she was desperate, and I was only gatecrashing it.
I was so nervous as I walked through the village, I concealed my face with the hood of my coat as I sat on the bench.

I could still feel the surge of adrenaline running through me, as I sat on the bench outside of a Woolworths store. It was then that

I felt a stern hand on my wrist, and as I turned, I looked on and saw Mrs. Belcher. The town's busy body was the worst person you would want to meet if you were on the run. "Maria Sweeney! What are you doing here? Shouldn`t you be in St Mary's house?" "Let go of me!" I shouted, angrily grabbing her wrist off my arm.

"Richard, look who it is, it's Maria, the Sweeney girl, quick call St Mary's!" she shouted.
"Your ugly evil bastard!" I shouted.
"How dare you speak to me like that!" she shouted. I desperately tried to escape but my efforts were a disaster.

One of the guard's cars had pulled up to where I was sitting, before I could escape the guards stood either side of me and forcefully dragged me into the car, as I watched the evil Mrs. Belcher, smiling, with an ugly smirk across her face. I was trembling in the car, on the way back to the asylum, I was terrified and worried about Sister Rita's wrath, it was a grave sin to attempt to leave the asylum, most girls who escaped were never caught and managed to live a life away from the asylum.
As I reached the asylum I looked on in horror as the guards dragged me down the corridor and pushed me inside a cold abandoned basement.

I felt at the time I would have preferred to have been punished by sister Rita and Sister Margaret, at least I would have known what to expect. I walked down the creaky steep wooden stairs, "Hello who is there?" asked a familiar voice, I recognized the voice as Rose. As I made my way to the bottom of the stairs a crack in the window allowed the light from the moon to shine on Rose's face. Rose's hands were tied by a rope to the wall, she had scratched on her face.

"Well, Rose I might have known you would be here there is no smoke without fire,"

"So, you're talking to me?"

"I have no choice Rose, why are you here?"

"I smashed my porridge on the floor, I tried to escape, and they chained me to the wall, why are you here?" she asked.

"I'm here Rose because you set fire to Sister Edgar's house, and I got the blame, everyone at home thinks I'm a crazed criminal."

"I'm so sorry I did admit it was me, but Sister Edgar was adamant that it was you, she is deranged you know that."

"I collapsed into a heap onto the floor, I lay down in desperation, "Rose, we have to find a way out of here without getting caught, I don't want to die here," I cried.

"We will find a way to steal the keys and escape, and I promise you Rita will suffer!" she squirmed.

Then in a moment of madness Rose found a rat crawling on the floor and proceeded to throw it at me, I grabbed the rat and threw it across the room.

"Your crazy bitch!" I shouted before we burst out into a fit of laughter.

CHAPTER 10:
SPORTS DAY

The following day Rose escorted me into her office and ordered Margaret to hurt me thirty times, I was emotionally drained after being awake all night. "That will teach you to defy us here at St Mary's," she growled. She sat so smug at her desk, her vacant cold stare never altered. As I arrived back into the dormitory the girls were delighted to see that I was back and that I was safe and well.

As I walked into the bathroom, I investigated the mirror and after six months of being in the asylum, I noticed a rapid decline in my physical appearance. I was skinny as a rake, my hair was greasy, my ankles were swollen, and I appeared to have gained deep varicose veins in my legs. I was exhausted and felt like I was losing hope.

The following day was a sports day, an event held once a year in the grand gardens of the asylum. The public was invited to watch, and included priests from local churches, teachers, and healthcare staff. The

nun's presented a very false view of what life was like in the asylum, they appeared supportive and humorous to the outside when they were devils in disguise. There was a range of activities that took place on the day, including the egg and spoon race, a running competition, and a
tunnel obstacle course. I was disgusted watching how different Sister Rita and Sister Margaret were, laughing and participating in the activities.

Many of the girls in the asylum took part, so I decided to sit in the field and watch rather than humiliate myself in front of the eyes of the public. I watched as the popular girls from my school sat in the center of the crowd watching. The ring reader Joanne Michaels sat in a green suit, her long blonde hair in perfect condition, covered in makeup, laughing at the girls, whilst they sat there with no worries. I was so jealous of Joanne and her friends, they had a future to look forward to, whilst all my dreams of going to medical school disintegrated in front of me.

CHAPTER 11:
CHRISTMAS

Christmas was the hardest time for me in the asylum. I always found Christmas to be a time of contemplation and reflection. Christmas with my parents and Bertie was such a special time. On Christmas Eve we would dress in Santa outfits and carry a sack of presents, and deliver them to local families, whilst singing Christmas carols on the doorstep.

On our patio driveway, my father set up a giant inflatable singing Santa Claus. The outside of our house was decorated with white Christmas lights. In the dining room, we had our grand ten-foot Christmas tree with hundreds of presents wrapped with a ribbon underneath. We would buy gifts not just for ourselves, but for the poorer families in our community. I truly missed Bertie and my parents at this time, my family had been torn apart and the happy memories slowly started to fade.

To the girls in the dormitory, it was just another day, we had a break from our work duties and could sit together in the dining room.

For our Christmas meal, we had a cold stale turkey dinner and for the pudding, we had an orange. We were already given an orange each in the morning as part of our present. In the front of the dining room on the top table was Margaret Rita and the other nun's eating their hot turkey dinner with steam coming from their food, whilst we struggled through our freezing dinner. It was cruel but It was the kind of behaviour I expected.

In the dining hall, the girls sat together and sang Christmas songs. I watched as Eileen taught Jane the 'Rudolph the red-nosed reindeer' song. Jane was so much more innocent than the other girls, she had never experienced being loved by a family, she never had friends to play with, and she had never ventured out of the gates of the asylum. Interacting with Jane was like seeing a small baby seeing the world through brand new eyes.

Each year we were given permission to write one letter to a family member and that afternoon I decided to write a letter to my mother.

Dear Mum,

It has now been over a year since I have seen you and Dad, and I wanted to write to you both. I understand you are both angry and ashamed at me, but you must know I did not start the fire at the nun's house, and I stand by that. Each day here gets more difficult than the last, my legs are sore, my feet ache and I collapse into a state of exhaustion at night. I miss school, I miss my friends and I miss my freedom. It is like a prison here, we are treated like criminals and I am innocent. So, I make a request to you both, please come and collect me and take me home, I do not care if I am punished, I just want to have the chance to have my life back. Please help me!

I am so sorry.

Maria

When I sent the letter, I was desperate for help, I always lived in hope that my parents would help me, but they had given up on me. I was fighting the battle on my own.

CHAPTER 12:
THE HERO

The Easter mass was another important event that seemed to be used as a show of alliance by the nuns, to fool the public that they were supporting the girls at St Mary's. For the Easter mass, we were given blue dresses to wear with a white shawl worn over their heads. The only positive part of the day was being able to walk two miles to St Thomas cathedral. The grand cathedral held over five hundred people, including family members of the girls in the asylums.

The events that occurred on the day of the Easter mass was about to start a chain reaction of negative events. It was a hot day and the sun scalded our skin, as we walked in two's with guards at the side of us to prevent the girls from escaping.

We arrived at the grand cathedral midday, and we had to prepare to sing 'Ave Maria' and 'Amazing Grace', two hymns we had practiced for over a month. We were worried as we knew the performance would have to be perfect, we wouldn't dare sing a note out of tune. As I sat next to Helen, I realized how nervous she was, her face was paler than usual, her hands were trembling, and tears filled her eyes. "Helen, what's wrong?" I asked.

"I can't take this anymore," she whispered. I held onto her hand tightly, to assure her that I supported her.

As we stood upon the altar for my performance, I could immediately see my parents standing at the back of the church. My mother was wearing a red dress and a red hat, whilst my father wore a grey suit and a top hat. I wondered if they had read my letter, I wondered as I stared at them, if there was any chance of them welcoming me back home. Both of my parents stood with vacant looks on their faces.

During the performance, I watched as Laura, a sixteen-year-old girl ran out of the cathedral in a desperate bid for freedom, although one of the guards ran after her, Laura was successful, she managed to escape that day and was never seen again.

After the mass, we made the long walk back to the asylum. I walked with Helen at the end of the line and felt very uneasy. I realized that Helen's behaviour had changed, she rarely spoke, she was very tearful and was nervous in her communication. I had also noticed that her weight had deteriorated. She was now six stone.

I felt it was my responsibility to help Helen as the nun's had no awareness of her deteriorating mental health issues. As we reached the bridge overlooking the crystal lake. In her weakest moment, Helen climbed onto the top of the bridge and dived into the sea. The girls gasped in terror, I knew I had to help her, and I pulled myself up to the bridge and dived in. The water was so cold it hit me like a knife, I shouted for Helen but there was no response. I frantically swam underneath and could see Helen falling lower into the sea, as I moved closer to pull her away, she pushed me back. So, I wrapped my arms around her and dragged her up to the sea, as our heads reached above the water, Helen hysterically began to cry. "Why did you save me? I wanted to die!" Helen screamed.

I could feel that Helen was giving up as I dragged her to the edge, and was met by an ambulance team, and the girls surrounded Helen, and the ambulance team checked her observations to ensure Helen was safe to return to the asylum. When we returned to the asylum, I wrapped several blankets around Helen, but she still was still shivering in the bed, crying hysterically for the rest of the evening.

I decided that I needed to make sister Rita listen to me to understand that Helen needed help and at 7 pm I knocked on Sister Rita's door. As I walked in, I could see her smoking her cigarette, "How can I help you with Maria?"
"It's Helen, Sister. I'm really worried about her. She is crying all the time, she's not eating, and she has entered this deep depressive state. Please Sister she needs a doctor"
"Are you a nurse or a medical professional?" She grunted.

"No sister,"

"You have no idea what you are talking about so please leave my office and go!" she shouted.

"Your sister was the same, always trying to interfere and that's what led to her demise." she groaned. I felt a shiver run through my spine and wondered if Sister Rita really knew Bertie's whereabouts.

I spent the following days monitoring Helen as the nun's refused to help her, I felt as if I had no choice but to protect her. After falling into the river Helen seemed more vacant and distant, she was so nervous and frightened around the other girls.

I had now been in the asylum for over a year and my character had changed. I started to become hardened and emotionally resilient to the cruel behavior of the nuns. On my 17th Birthday I thought about the life I was missing, I felt I should have been out looking at colleges and studying for my medical exams. I spent my 17th birthday scrubbing the halls of the asylum, with a large bucket of water and a damp cloth, with Katlynn. I felt my knees graze across the surface of the floor, my elbows were tired and had a deep cut from leaning on the floor, and my back would ache deeply. Kaitlynn had now seemed to take over the role of Dawn as the mother figure, she would shout at me if I missed a spot of dust whilst cleaning the floor and would take out her frustration on the other girls. I had missed Rose, the nun had noticed we had a close relationship and worked very hard to keep us apart, making sure we were in separate rooms and that we were not left alone. Sister Rita was suspicious of us and with good reason, I knew she feared we were going to escape, and we were determined to leave.

That afternoon I walked up to the dormitory and filled my basin with warm water. My legs were still bleeding, and I would constantly reapply plasters to open wounds. That afternoon at 7 pm we received a knock on the door: it was Kaitlyn's father. He stormed into the dormitory angrily in his black suit and rusty suitcase, He had tanned skin and he looked at us sternly.
"Father, what are you doing here?"
"Your stepmother has passed, and we are moving to England, pack your things we are leaving today," He groaned.
I watched as he stood expressionless with his arms folded before waiting outside of the dormitory. Katelynn appeared with a shocked expression on her face. We watched her pack her suitcase with jealousy and wonder. We all had dreamed and thought about being collected from the asylum. I had never built a relationship with Katelynn, but I was sad to see her go.

"Good luck girls and keep strong I'll be back ok one day to watch this building burn down." she smiled. It was then that we watched her leave with her anxious father. I hoped that she would find peace with her family since her mother's passing.

Later in the evening, I became concerned as Helen had been missing for over an hour. The girls in the dormitory had noticed that the bathroom door had been bolted shut. I called out for Helen, but there was no answer, so I kicked open the door knocking the chair onto the floor. As I looked inside, I stood in shock and let out a scream. Helen had hanged herself from a rope to the chandelier in the bathroom. I desperately unhooked the rope and Helen fell to the floor. I held her lifeless body, knowing that she was dead, as tears fell down my face. In a strange way she looked in peace, all the worry, anguish, and despair had disappeared from her face. Eileen and Jane walked into the room and collapsed in shock, whilst Sister Margaret stood at the door in shock, before kneeling to the ground.

I tried for so long to encourage the nuns to help Helen and expressed that she had mental health needs, but they ignored my pleas. The nuns had let us all down, but most of all Helen.

I suddenly felt so much guilt, I should have watched her more closely, I should have protected her. It was then that I watched as tears fell from Sister Margaret's face, it was the first sign of humanity she had shown since I entered the asylum, maybe there was hope for her yet.

CHAPTER 13: REBELLION

I was so distraught after Helen passed away, I had so much guilt and I finally felt like I was defeated by the nun's, I could not see a way out of the asylum, and I fell into a deep sea of depression. My severe depression had affected my appetite, I couldn't sleep, I couldn't talk, I had lost interest in everything. I was once a carefree, spoiled teenager from a privileged background, I was now a faceless girl, we were not treated as individuals, we were criminals.

At mealtime, I would take a few bites of the food and put the rest of the food in my pockets before disposing of it out of the window. I had refused to speak to Eileen and Jane and the other girls, my only friend was my journal. I had spent two months living in a manic-depressive state before a catalyst event changed everything.

I woke up on a warm summer's day in June, it was so hot in the workroom, I could feel the sweat pouring off me as I leaned over the large basin. I had now become transfixed on my work, and felt almost robotic in my approach, washing the sheets, folding them and then leaving them out to dry. At lunchtime I sneaked upstairs into the dormitory to rest on the bed for a half an hour, I had so little energy.

When I looked out of the window through the stained-glass window, I could see a shadowy figure standing at the gate, with a hat and sunglasses. I wondered if it was Bertie coming to see me, I often wondered if one day she would come and collect me, even though a part of me felt she died. Sometimes when I looked out of the window, I believed I could see my father standing angrily by the gate, holding onto his suitcase looking on in contempt. When I told Dawn about my family members, she described this as a hallucination and believed we could see what we wanted to see.

That afternoon, I was so exhausted that I fell asleep through my lunch break and was awoken by Rose who squeezed my hand. She sat next to me under the window. "Where have you been? I've been looking for you everywhere. Even though you haven't spoken in months I still watch you everyday. Maria, you must eat, you must keep your strength up, you look like death, plus we are not giving up without a fight. We will leave this hell and we will live a normal life again." Rose smiled.

I could barely see Rosie, my vision was blurry, and I felt so faint. I realized I had to put up a fight and try to keep my head above the

depression I was under. Rose took me by the hand, and we made our way to the dining hall. As I sat down for the evening meal, I struggled to eat the cold lumpy mash and vegetables. Then as I gazed at Rose smiling at me, I grabbed the mash and threw it at her. This caused Rose to throw her chocolate dessert at me. Soon the other girls followed in unison and a manic food fight erupted and the dining room transformed into a sea of colorful mess. The food fight came to a dramatic halt when Sister Margaret came into the room. "Stop" she roared, but it was too late, she had witnessed me throwing the last spoonful. "Maria, come to my office now!" Rita roared

When I reached the office, I was forced to the floor where Sister Rita performed her vicious attack. "For two months you have not spoken, and now you choose to throw sacred food around the hall!"

"Sister, I told you Helen needed help, no one listened to me!"

She began cutting my hair viciously leading to a deep bloody cut, before taking a razor and shaving my head completely. I was stripped of my femininity. I looked in the mirror and I felt numb with emotion but knew from that moment on I would have to take revenge. The guards escorted me to the cellar, and I spent the night huddled against the stone-cold wall, whilst the rats scurried around my feet. I thought about what I would do to Sister Rita to exact revenge, I thought of throwing the boiling water in the laundry basin over her, or throwing a fresh large amount of horse manure over her to show her how humiliation feels.

The following morning, I retired to the dormitory, and the girls looked on in shock at my unsightly new appearance. "Oh, Maria, you look like a gangster criminal with the new haircut."

"Shut up Eileen at least I don't have your ugly face!" I scowled. It was then that Jane ran up to me and gave me a hug, "I'm so glad you're talking again I missed you."

"Maria, I need to speak to you, in private, "Eileen murmured. I walked with Eileen to the bathroom and we sat down on the cold banister.

"Helen left a suicide note under her pillow, Sister Rita tried to hide it, but when Sister Margaret was doing her room checks, she found it under the floorboard.

"Maria she said she could not put up with the treatment anymore and she explained that Father Michael was a monster and had been making sexual advances to her, and she witnessed one girl in a room with him and he was kissing her, and she put in the letter that he threatened to kill

her if she told anyone. Maria the girl he kissed was Jane," Eileen whispered.

"Oh god that is awful, what did they do with the letter?"

"Sister Rita ripped up in front of me even though it was addressed to her father, and she said if I spoke a word of it, she would make sure I had a permanent residency in the cellar," Eileen cried.

"I will make them pay for this one day, they drove her to suicide, she had no choice," I sighed.

That morning I enjoyed my porridge in the morning, after deciding it was time for me to give up my fasting and to start eating again. At breakfast time Sister Rita would always stand with her arms folded, lucking at us angrily, ready to attack like a bulldog. In the dining room was a new nun, a nineteen-year-old nun called Jenny. Jenny appeared different to the other nun's. She was pretty with long blond hair, olive skin, and bright blue kind eyes. Jenny did not seem to fit in with Margaret and Rita.

I was fully focused on my escape plan with Rose, I had spent nearly two years in the asylum, and I could not risk my mental health deteriorating

any further. I observed how hardworking and diligent Rose had become offering to help the nuns at any opportunity. Rose would often be seen asking to wash extra sheets and agreeing to scrub the floors for the nuns.

At break time I sat out in the courtyard with Rose, the sun was so bright, the heat against our neck almost scalded us. That's the guard, James he is our key to get out of here," she smiled. James was six-foot-tall tanned with curly blonde hair.
"He seems to like me, so I can trick him and steal the key, he has already invited me for tea in the private dormitory upstairs."
"Well that is positive news, but we must not get caught, this time I need to say goodbye to this wretched place."
"It has to be early at 6am, as that is when O'Leary's delivery van arrives.

"You girls are planning your big escape plan?" muttered a voice behind us. The girl was Clara Rollins, she was sixteen five foot one, with freckles and her red hair was in plaits.

"Keep out of our business your fat ugly bitch," Rose sniped.
Clara ushered us to one side and told us the story of the group of girls who had escaped the asylum five years ago. The group of ten girls were led by Jean Avery, a defiant girl who had spent seven years in the asylum. Jane claimed she was burnt on her back by Sister Rita's iron.

She conjured a courageous escape plan, her friend on the outside was able to give her several sleeping tablets to drug the nun's and guards. Jean was successful in her plan and once the guards succumbed to the sleeping tablets. Ten of the girls charged outside of the asylum with their sticks lit up with fire. The girls were never to be found again, the nuns saw this as a travesty, and to prevent this from happening again they attached metal spikes and barbed wire to other gates, to prevent such a catastrophe from happening.

That afternoon I was confident in Rose's escape plan and finally felt I could look with hope into the future. In the evenings after a long shift at work, I would relax in my room and paint on the pieces of paper left by Bertie. I had been working on a painting of the view of my family cottage
from the sunset cornfield. Beside the cottage was a magnificent wind turbine, and in the garden of our house was our magnificent treehouse, filled with posters of Elvis and Frank Sinatra. Inside the treehouse, we had a telescope and at night we would look out and make our wishes for the future. We had a privileged life as children; we did not know that our happy life would be a long distant memory.

CHAPTER 14: ROAD TO FREEDOM

Two months had passed since I was viciously attacked by Sister Margaret in the asylum. My hair started to grow back, and we were only a week away from undertaking our escape plan. I had changed my behavior to fool the nuns. I would volunteer to lead prayers every morning, ask for extra duties, and even bow down to Sister Margaret. It was all part of my plan to fool her and the other nun's that I was abiding by the rules.

I discussed with Rose in-depth our escape plan in fine detail. We planned to take the Ferry to London, upon arrival if we were to make it, we would stay with Rose's cousin, who is a trained hairdresser, and we hoped to gain work in the salon. I had planned to go to the papers and shout from the rooftops about all the cruel treatment I endured.

On Sunday afternoon Sister Rita gave me a letter to deliver personally to Father Michael along with a basket of fruit, "Oh sister Rita, I hope to be as gracious as you one day, when I become a nun." "Oh, Maria I never thought I would hear you say that you know you've really turned a corner," she smiled. I was shocked at her gullibility, and that she believed my bullshit excuse.

I walked over to the courtyard of the church, and when I entered the church, I noticed how unusually quiet it was. The church inside was beautiful with bright red carpet, and stained-glass windows depicting the stations of the cross. The altar was golden, and at either side of the altar were two magnificent flower beds filled with red roses. At this point the church had lost all religious meaning for me, the actions of the nun's and the priests had made me dissociate myself from the catholic religion.

As I walked nervously down the aisle, I could hear muffled voices in the reception room. I tiptoed towards the door but was very aware of Father Michael's temper, so I was careful not to disturb him if he was in a meeting. I knelt with the basket of fruit and as I looked through the keyhole, I held my breath in shock. I witnessed Father Michael and Jane from my dormitory in a passionate embrace. I could not breathe, in shock, I dropped the fruit basket on the floor. I ran down the aisle as fast as I could, I could hear Father Michael shouting, "who is it?" I ran as fast as I could out of the church courtyard, I could hear Father Michael's heavy footsteps coming behind me.

I felt like my heart was going to explode. In a panic, I hid behind a towering bush. I observed a red-faced Father Michael looking angry and frustrated. Sweat poured from his face and I observed him nervously walk back towards the church.

I felt so angry at what I saw, it confirmed to me that Eileen was telling the truth. I was determined to not let Jane meet the same fate as Helen. I wanted her to join me and Rose on our escape plan. I had to help her. I had an obligation.

The day after I witnessed the event was one of the most peaceful days in the asylum. Sister Margaret and Sister Rita were attending a meeting in Donegal, leaving Sister Jenny in charge. Sister Jenny was so calm and caring, she was new to working in the asylum, but she encouraged us to talk to each other and to interact. It was almost as if she was the 'supply teacher,' we could do what we wanted.

I sat with Rose in the dining room to tell her about my idea and what I witnessed in the church. "We have to get Jane out of the

asylum, they will kill her and if I leave her, I will have blood on my hands."
"Are you crazy? She is a loaded gun, she is crazy as a fruit, she is not strong enough, she can't go with us!" Rose persisted.
"If she doesn't join us you're on your own," I exclaimed.

It was such a wonderful day in the asylum. In the laundry room, Sister Jenny helped us wash the linen, and we could have an extended break in the courtyard for over an hour long. In the evening Sister Jenny put on the wireless radio in the dining room tour enjoyment. That evening we
danced To Elvis Presley, Frank Sinatra, and the Beatles. I stood in awe looking around at the other girls in the asylum, the girls were smiling and laughing. I had never felt so happy, it felt wonderful to finally let go. Then at 7 pm, our perfect evening was crushed. Sister Rita came storming into the dormitory and grabbed the plug from the socket of the radio. "What on earth is going on? Girls go to your dormitories in an orderly fashion in this instance. I washed as Sister Rita bore her evil green eyes into poor sister Jenny who stood trembling with fear.

The day after, whilst I was in the courtyard a young girl was standing by the garden gate entrance. She stood in her black suit, her hair was wild and curly, I recognized her as a school friend of Bertie, her name was Hayley. I walked over to her as the rain started to pour, I trembled as the cold rain soaked me through. "Oh Maria, I have a message for you. It's Bertie, she is a student in London, at the bank hospital, she wanted you to know where she is," she smiled. Hayley then passed the wet soaked note, I ran towards Rose's dormitory, and found her laying on the bed looking through an old brown scrapbook.
"Oh Rose I have the best news, Bertie is safe, she is working as a student doctor in London!" We have to find her!" I beamed.

Rose was so engrossed in the scrapbook that she seemed to ignore what I had said. The scrapbook was stolen from Sister Rita's office, it detailed all of the girls who had entered the asylum, including evidence of written punishments given by the nun's.

"What are you doing? You have to put it back, Sister Rita will go berserk!" I shouted.

"She will never find out, we are taking this book with us when we leave, we are taking them down once and for all!" she smiled.

A week slowly passed in the asylum, and I was a nervous wreck, slowly anticipating the day of our escape, and the day before we were to escape it felt like our plan was fully coming together. It took me two hours to convince Jane that leaving the asylum was in her best interests and would help to improve her life. Rose had given us each a plank of wood that we hid under the bed, to use for ammunition if we are caught by the guards.

I spent the entire night listening to the howling of the wind, as the moon shined directly on my face. I felt a mixture of emotions that night, I was excited, nervous, and filled with fear over the prospect of escaping. I knew now that it was now or never, I could not spend another day in the asylum, being treated like a slave. I was ready to use reasonable force to escape the clutches of the guards and the nuns. I wanted to experience freedom and I was willing to put up the fight of my life.

CHAPTER 15: GOING TO BATTLE

At 6 am I sat up in the bed listening to the calming sound of the birds singing in the sycamore trees. I stood by the window and overlooked the beautiful mountains in the distance. An eerie misty fog danced across the mountain tops, as the bright sun reflected off the window penetrating my eyes. I stood in the bathroom and looked on in fear, I began to stand tall and I took several short breaths, before clenching my fists, and I was ready to go.

As I left the room, Jane was dressed in her blue petticoat, holding her satchel across her chest. "Now Jane you mustn't make a sound, if they catch us, we will be in very serious trouble," I warned. I was trying to be brave when inside of me was a frightened child wanting to steam out.

"Let's go" I whispered, giving Jane a nervous shaky smile. Both of us held onto our large planks of wood, and we tiptoed with apprehension across the creaky floorboard. As we left the dormitory, we slowly walked down the spiral stairs.

There was silence all around us, you could hear a pin drop. I was so nervous my whole body was shaking, and I cried with fear. I was so concerned for Jane, she was a loose cannon, if anyone was to foil our plan or act irrationally it would be Jane.

At the bottom of the spiral staircase, standing with her large plank of the wood was a brave and defiant Rose. She stood with a devilish smile on her face, she looked so brave and determined to fight. We all stood together at the bottom of the stairs overlooking the long and winding corridor which would lead us to freedom, we focused solely on the steel door, as Rose held onto the silver keys. We ran down the hall and reached the door, Rose was so nervous that her hand was trembling as she attempted to open the door, finally managing after the third try.

"Woohoo we did it!" shouted Jane.

"Your stupid bitch be quiet!" Rose hissed.

Suddenly the six-foot guard Derek walked out of his sleeping quarters, "what is going on?" he shouted. Suddenly Rose hit him on the head with great force, knocking him unconscious on the floor. Then to our great horror sister Rita followed, in her nightdress, her face filled with rage.

She charged towards me and it was then with great force that I punched her face, causing her to fall, I watched as she fell to the ground, and kicked her in anger, "You evil bitch!" I shouted. I watched as she looked up at me in terror, before she let out a terrifying scream, "Help" she shouted.

Suddenly three guards appeared from the end of the corridor charging towards us, one of them grabbed Jane. As we exited through the front door Rose shut the front door and began to lock it. "What are you doing? We can't leave Jane inside!" I shouted.
"Shut up!" Rose roared. She took my hand and we ran towards the steel gates, prized them open, and there it was the O'Leary truck about to pull off.

We quickly prized ourselves into the back of the truck filled with flour and other food sources. We lay down, covering ourselves in a grey sheet covering. We could hear the guards unlock the door. I had never been so scared, I felt like my heart was going to explode. I had physically assaulted Sister Rita. I would not survive this if I was caught.

Rose held onto my hand and started to grip onto it tightly, "We will be ok, we are safe," she whispered. It was then that the driver pulled off.
We could hear Sister Rita hobble onto the road with the guards, crying out to the guards in pain.
"You need to get those girls and bring them back as soon as possible! This was attempted murder that witch nearly killed me!" he screamed.
In the distance, we could hear the guards scurry towards their

cars.

As I lay in the back of the trunk, I had never felt so much fear and relief at the same time. We were about to head into the unknown and I was petrified. I felt exhausted already as I observed the swaying of the branches as we zoomed through the busy country road. I watched as the seagulls swooped above our heads. An hour later we arrived in Dublin and we quickly hopped out of the van, and ran down the road being careful to avoid the attention of the driver.

Rose ushered me into the Marks and Spencer store, we looked like stowaways in our dirty muddy clothes. The uptown women in their petticoats and hats looked at us with disgust.

"Rose, we should keep going, there is no time for shopping, they are after us!" I shouted.
"No, we need a disguise if we are going to truly escape the guards will stop at nothing to find us," Rose exclaimed.
"You have no money to buy clothes!" I whispered.
It was then that Rose lifted three hundred dollars out of her over-coat that she had stolen from the safe. We both bought ourselves two business suits with large black oval sunglasses and a grand oval summer hat.

As we looked at each other in the mirror after getting changed we instantly looked unrecognizable. We were no longer the asylum girls, we were free. It felt so great to wear sunglasses and a hat, I felt so comfortable hiding away from people. After being in the asylum for over two years I had such low self-esteem, I felt as if the public hated us and looked at us as outcasts and that's just how we felt.

Rose grabbed my hand and she walked towards the cinema, and we bought a ticket to watch Calamity jane. "Are you crazy we can't watch a film at a time like this!" I warned her. "We have a few hours to kill before the ferry leaves, we can, and we will watch the film!" Rose cheered.

We walked into the theatre and sat on the red leather seats and shared a large bucket of sweet popcorn.

"This is crazy, the guards will be looking for us," I stammered.

"They will never find us now and we are in disguise. It felt wonderful to be free, I expected the nuns to creep behind me and order me back to the asylum. As we watched the film, we danced, we sang along, and we threw our popcorn in the air in defiance. After the cinema, we shared a packet of fish and chips. As we walked down the busy high street, we relished our first hot meal in two years. I felt so comfortable walking with the oval shades covering my face, I felt it helped me hide away from people, hide away from judgment.

"Maybe I can get the train tomorrow back to Enniskillen, there must be some way I can make my parents understand, somehow I need to make them listen."

"Oh Jesus Christ Maria you need to get over this, you cannot see your parents again, they have had you condemned, they will never trust you again, you saw that when your mother abandoned you at the gates, you have to find your own path now, you have no choice," Rose shouted.

I started to burst out crying hysterically, I felt that there was no hope left for me, I always wanted a connection with my family, but I felt like I was heading into the world alone. That afternoon before we headed off to the dock top to catch our ferry, we headed to the beach. We stood on the rocky hilltop, overlooking the crystal blue sea. "C'mon Maria we need to jump into the sea!" "You're crazy, we can't!" I stammered. Rose grabbed my hand and we ran before jumping into the freezing sea. It felt wonderful to swim in the sea, it was the ultimate sign of freedom. Above us, we could see the seagulls sweeping above us, as the sun cast a shadow over our faces.

At 7pm we headed onto the ferry on our way to England to start our new life. We set off along the rough Irish sea and made our way to our small cabin room with two camper beds. We were so nervous we could not sleep. We both slept under our large wool overcoats, I was determined to be happy in England and to find Bertie so that I would not feel alone.

CHAPTER 16: LONDON

We arrived in London at 5am, the next day and took a coach to London, and we arrived at Marylebone station at 8 am that morning. I felt so underdressed in our bland brown overcoats. The train was full of men and women, rushing through the station to get onto their train. The men were dressed in their waistcoats and suits, whilst the women were dressed in bright beautiful summer dresses, looking like models I would only see in a magazine. I found myself standing in the train station, bewildered, and in awe at the sights around me. I could sell the smell of the fresh hot chocolate in the coffee shop and the sounds of the train conductor blowing the whistle, and as we left the train station, we were consumed by the cloud of smoke from the cars on the high-street.

Rose whistled for a taxi and we jumped into a yellow taxi, "to Paddington station," she ordered. I was so excited I felt like a child again, I put the windows down and screamed, my hair blew in the wind.

I marveled at the magnificent town hall buildings, and Rose took a picture of Big Ben, and I embraced her in the car.
"Thank you so much for taking me here, for helping me to escape," I beamed.
"No problem, it's the first time I've seen you smile in so long, but we still have to be careful, we are on the run."
An hour later we arrived at Rose's cousin's house in Paddington, Rose's cousin was called Patricia. She lived in a two-story townhouse with her husband Eric. Patricia worked as a hairdresser, whilst Eric worked as a GP in the local doctor's surgery.
"Oh my God it's wonderful to see you Rose, I knew you would escape my little firecracker," she beamed. Patricia was very pretty, she was six-foot-tall and wore a bright blue gown, and her black hair towered above her head like a beehive.
"I'm Maria, a friend of Rose," I blurted out, nervously. Patricia showed us around her beautiful townhouse. The dining room had a king-size sofa, and a wide glass table, with gold chairs. The conservatory led to the large spacious garden, with a small swimming pool. Upstairs were four spacious guest rooms, and then she showed us our room in the attic with

bunk beds, covered in dust.

"This room will suit you both fine once you get on your feet, you can find a place of your own." Patricia smiled.
"So, we can start at the salon tomorrow?" I asked.
"Yes of course you can start from 12 pm tomorrow for light cleaning duties and then every other day I need you to arrive by 9 am. Ok, girl's me and Eric are going for dinner," I'll see you soon.

"It's not much of a room is it?" I complained.
"Maybe not but what do you expect of the Hilton, it will take awhile before we get on our feet." she smiled.
I was so tired that night I collapsed onto the bunk bed, I was exhausted from the long journey. I could smell the fresh sheets, I felt so peaceful and safe as I listened to the rain dance against the window ledge. Before I went to sleep that night, I thought about Jane alone in the cellar of the asylum, with no one to talk to and feeling alone. I imagined one day when I had enough money saved, I would help her escape.

The next day when I awoke, I walked downstairs to the kitchen, I made myself pancakes drizzled in golden syrup. As I sat down at the breakfast table, I felt something licking my feet, it was Patrica's rottweiler puppy. I jumped in horror and ran into the dining room. Rose came down and looked startled, "How can you be scared of a harmless dog your silly bitch," Rose exclaimed.

It was then that we made our way to Patricia's luxury salon which had a hairdressing station, jacuzzi, and swirl pool. I felt so embarrassed as I started cleaning the floors, whilst the high-class women getting their haircut referred to me as the 'maid.' My confidence was at an all-time low, I could barely lift my head up. "Maria you better smile or we'll lose customers." Rose stammered.

After the salon, I walked down the cobbled High Street and had a warm hot chocolate and cheese sandwich from the cafe rouge. All the people around me were rushing past on their lunch break, but I felt so paranoid I

felt like they were watching me and passing judgment. I was so paranoid, and I pulled the hood over my head to conceal my identity.

As I walked past, I reached the Jefferson Education center and enrolled into the biology lecture. Before the enrollment began, I walked into a hall that was filled with young teenagers, talking and enjoying the refreshments. I sat down on the table next to a tall tanned guy in a suit with blond sandy hair and emerald eyes, called Darren. The girl sitting next to him was Lorraine. She was pretty as a model, with long curly blonde hair, and brilliant blue eyes. Darren and Lorraine explained that they hoped to go to medical school. When they asked me about my past I froze. I could not tell them the truth.

"I'm Maria, I'm from Ireland, I've just graduated from high school, I live in Richmond street in Paddington with my parents."
"Oh, I love the house on Richmond street you are so lucky!" Lorraine beamed. We then spoke about our interest and Darren shared my interest in art and popular music. Then my worst nightmare occurred, my ID card from St Mary's asylum fell to the floor."

It revealed my identity as the 'asylum girl' and detailed who to contact if the card was found. I was distraught as Lorraine picked up the card, her expression turned from happiness to disgust. In a panic, I ran out of the center, and back to the townhouse. As I sat in the attic room, I could feel my heart racing against my chest, I was having a panic attack, I knew I would carry the stigma of being in the asylum everywhere I went.

The following week I tried so hard to fit into my new life in London. Patricia had been so kind to see and had given both us one hundred pounds, personal allowance, to help us with our living expenses over the following month. I bought myself a fur mink coat with a large hood to cover my face, which was already concealed by my sunglasses. Eric would work long hours and return home at 9 pm. Louise would cook us luxury meals including, pasta bake, roast dinners, and hot curries. It felt wonderful to have hot meals, in the asylum the meals were always cold and undercooked.

In my breaks from the salon, I would go window shopping in Harrods and the local food shops. I would see mothers sitting with their daughters at Cafe's, families sitting in restaurants, and families buying tickets for the movie show. I missed having a family connection.

One day everything was about to change, a change that would force me to change direction in my life.

It was a busy shift at the salon, and we were taking our final bookings for Christmas as the salon was due to close. As we swept the mountain heap of hair on the floor, Patricia stormed towards us.

"Girls, I have an urgent meeting at Canary Wharf, I'm going to have to postpone my final too meetings, hand them a discount card and have this place spotless before you leave," she muttered.

As soon as Patricia left Rose used a range of hair products on her hair including spray and moose. "Rose don't use these products you will get in trouble," I warned. It was then that Rose grabbed the booking form, "Oh I've just had a great idea, we should pre-

tend we are the hairdressers, Mrs. Windsor and her daughter are super-rich they will pay us well!" Rose beamed.
"We can't Patricia will fire us, we can't risk this!" I warned her.
"She'll never know, and anyway they are only after a trim.

Ten minutes later, Mrs. Windsor and her daughter Alana entered and they were the snottiest rudest people I ever met. Mrs. Windsor wore a pink

overcoat and her grand blue oval hat sat on top of her wild grey curly hair. Whilst Alana was a spoilt brat and sat in her blue dungarees and long blonde hair, boasting to Rose about her extravagant lifestyle of lavish parties and her one hundred boyfriends.
Rose began to cut Alana's hair, whilst I prepared the area for Mrs. Windsor.
"Oh, you must be Patrice's new assistant, just a tidy up and a few inches off the top." she beamed. I watched as Mrs. Windsor closed her eyes as I began to shake as I held the scissors in my hand. I nervously began to cut her hair, each cut was a lethal destruction to her hair. Mrs. Windsor was starting to resemble a scarecrow, whilst I watched as Rose cut Alana's hair intricately, in a professional way.
It was then that disaster struck. I knocked the electric razor on the floor, as I picked it up, I accidentally flicked the switch, causing it to turn on, and I accidentally cut off a huge chunk of Mrs. Windsor's hair, leaving a bald patch. I looked on in horror, before running out of the salon, whilst I heard the screams of Mrs. Windsor echoing through the window.
I pretended I was asleep that night as I could hear Patricia shouting at Rose, whilst I closed my eyes in the bed hoping Patricia would not call the staff in the asylum to collect us.

The next morning, as I walked down the wooden staircase, I could hear Patricia and Eric arguing in the kitchen. "I knew this was a bad idea, Patricia, you invite those two hooligans to the house and now this incident happens, it makes me think who really was responsible for the arson at the nun's home, maybe Rose was innocent all along."

"Maria was just nervous, that's all," Patricia added.
"Tell that to the lawyers when Mrs. Windsor Sue's us, either Maria goes tonight, or I'll throw her out!" he warned.
I ran upstairs and quietly packed my satchel as Rose lay snoring on the top bunk. I decided to get a train to Oxford, I needed to see Bertie, I needed to live my life with a purpose, I seeked a sense of belonging.

CHAPTER 17:
FINDING BERTIE

I jumped onto the steam drain at 10 am to Oxford, I knew that if I stayed with Bertie in Oxford, I would have security, and I wouldn't feel so alone.

It was a beautiful sunny day, I looked out of the window at the crops that glistened in the sun glow. On the train, I had a cheese salad sandwich. It felt wonderful to eat healthy food. In the asylum, we were forced to eat food rich in fat and sugar. I felt paranoid all the time. I convinced myself that everyone on the train was looking at me or whispering. In the asylum, I was always under a microscope.

I arrived in Oxford at 11 am, and took a taxicab to the medical school hall of residence. As I entered the reception, I witnessed a large group of medical students sitting at the university bar, in their white coats.

"Hi everyone, I'm looking for Bertie Sweeney, does anyone here know her?" I asked. The group of students all looked at me in surprise. Then a lady with short brown hair and green eyes stood up and walked towards me.

"I know Bertie has been my housemate for the past year, I'm Megan."

"Hi Megan, I'm Maria. I'm Bertie's sister."

"Hello Maria, I've heard so much about you, Bertie said you resided at one of the Magdalene asylums in her hometown-"

"Well, that is in the past," I groaned.

"Well come with me I will take you up to her room we can speak more up there," she smiled.

I walked with Megan up the rusty stairs, up the six flights of stairs and we made it to Bertie's room. I looked in wonder at Bertie's room. Bertie's room was filled with posters she had drawn, one was a picture of her at the asylum in the courtyard in her work clothes, holding onto the steel gates in desperation. Another artistic drawing was a picture of me and Bertie running through the golden crop field in our back garden. I felt like the picture symbolized freedom and showed that we had a life outside of the asylum.

"Bertie is quite the artist!" Megan smiled.

"In our hometown in Ireland she would spend hours drawing, she was the best artist I ever met. So, tell me where is Bertie? Is she working?" I asked.

"Well she's at St Thomas hospital, but you can't go there, there is something you need to know," She shouted.

It was too late ,I was so excited at knowing Bertie's whereabouts that I went outside and called a taxi and made my way to the hospital. As I reached the hospital reception, I asked the receptionist if she could locate Bertie for me. After five minutes, she explained that she was on ward 5b on the second floor. I ran upstairs and excitedly made my way through the acute medical ward, looking around for Bertie in her white doctors' uniform as a trainee doctor.

I reached the nurse's station and saw a stern-looking doctor with wild curly hair and dark-rimmed glasses. "Hi Sir, I'm looking for Bertie Sweeny, a colleague of yours."
"Bertie is a patient inside room one." he groaned, refusing to look at me.
I nervously walked to the side room, and in the cold clinical room was Bertie laying in the hospital bed, her face was pale, with bags under her eyes, she held onto her oxygen mask on her face, her hair was curly and greasy. She was covered in her rainbow blanket. She looked so sick, and as she lifted the oxygen mask from her mouth, tears slowly fell from her face. "I can't believe it, you escaped, you found me!" she cried.

I knelt beside Bertie on the bed and looked on in awe, she looked so tired, every breath and spoken word felt like such an exhausting effort. "I thought you would be working, I would never have imagined you were a patient here, what's wrong Bertie?" I asked, holding onto her hand tightly.

"A few months ago I was working a student on the labor ward, and halfway through the shift I collapsed in pain, I was rushed to the hospital and had blood tests and a scan, three weeks later I was diagnosed with bladder cancer," she murmured, as her hand started to tremble in mine.

"You're going to be ok though Bertie, you're young, you're 20, you will fight this illness." I pleaded.

"I wish that was true, at first the consultant stated it was treatable, but I had surgery two weeks ago to remove the tumor, and later discovered that the cancer has spread." she cried.

I started crying hysterically, as I held onto both of her hands, "we will make it through this we have to," I shouted.

It was then that Bertie sat up in the bed and slowly shuffled to the edge, I watched as she struggled. "Listen, Maria, there is no easy way to say this, but I'm going to die, the doctor has given me three months to live, I want to live my final days in peace, but I'm so glad that you're here with me and that I won't feel alone." she smiled, through her deep tears.

That afternoon, I discussed life in the asylum with Bertie and explained the escape plan to her, and my disastrous trip to London. I was so thankful that Bertie offered me a place to stay in her halls of residence, whilst she continued her treatment in hospital, and she explained we would rent a cottage to live out her final months. I slowly walked out of the hospital in shock, I felt so depressed, I felt like I was cursed and destined to live my life on my own. I knew that night that I had to be strong for Bertie.
Every day I would visit Bertie in the hospital, and I would watch with sadness at how weak she would become. In the mornings, I would help her walk to the bathroom, and to assist her with a wash every morning. After her chemotherapy, I would prepare Bertie's art table and we would spend the afternoon drawing and paint together.

Two weeks later, Bertie was discharged from hospital, and we rented a beautiful cottage, hidden behind a rose bush on a derelict country road. The cottage was spacious, inside was a red sofa covered in a patchwork quilt, and hanging on the wall was a golden grandfather clock. The kitchen had black and white Edwardian tiles and a round table. The garden overlooked a ten-acre field. As soon as we walked outside, we were greeted by the Robins and falcons, and in the summer heat, we would sleep to the singing of the bird, and the choir of crickets. I slept in the guest room, whilst Bertie slept in the master suite, overlooking the field and mountains in the distance. In the room, I hung up several of Bertie's paintings including the picture of our childhood home.

The first day in the cottage was perfect, at 9 am we sat at the oak table and ate pancakes with golden syrup. Then after the nurse came to administrate her tablets, we listened to our favourite Elvis and Frank Sinatra songs, and then at Lunch, we would lay back on the deck table and soak up the rays. This afternoon, Bertie passed a small brown package over to me. Inside was a nursing student application form with details of the nursing halls of residence.

"What is this for?" I asked

"It's a plan for the future Maria when I'm gone, I want you to apply for the nursing course, you will meet new people and gain a range of new experiences. I want to know that when I'm gone you have a plan for your future." she smiled.

"Let's not talk about that now, I've had no family for two years, I'm enjoying this time," I exclaimed.

"Just promise me you'll look!" she warned.

I had not thought about my career, so many of my dreams died when I walked into the asylum. The next day I went to St Thomas hospital, and I observed through the window the student nurses, sitting around a table practicing their injection technique on an orange. The nurses were dressed in blue dresses and a white hat. The nurses lived together and had meals provided for them. Nursing was a respectable career for girls, and many started their journey at seventeen, leaving behind their childhood home, and starting on the road to independence.

It was now December, and it was the most perfect weather. I watched in awe as I woke up on Christmas Eve to the tower of snow in the field. I stepped outside of our cottage, and looked up as the snowflakes fell onto me, all around me was silence. The cottage resembled a giant snow globe with only the windows visible. In the dining room was our six-foot Christmas tree, decorated in red baubles. Under the tree, I wrapped up several presents in red wrapping paper tied with a golden ribbon. I bought Bertie her favorite chocolates, an Elvis record, and her favorite board games. On the ceiling I attached a red tinsel, and I placed a red tablecloth on the oval oak table with jewelry hidden in the self-made Christmas crackers.

Bertie's illness progressed quickly following discharge from hospital, she became weaker each day, she could only walk short distances, and I helped her with eating, and assisted her in her wash and dressing each day.

However early in the morning, I started to panic as I could not find her in her room and the front door was open. As I walked outside, I found Bertie kneeling in her green overcoat next to a five-foot snowman she had created as a child, with a multicolored scarf around his neck.

"Bertie are you crazy? You will catch a cold! Get inside!" I shouted.

It's so funny Maria, for years I wished for it to snow at Christmas, and here we are in the final months of my life surrounded by snow."

We then walked inside the cottage and sat by the log fire watching our favourite Christmas films, the wizard of oz, and 'it's a wonderful life.' We felt nostalgic, remembering singing the songs together as a family, and remembering how the mother would cry at the end of both films.

After lunch, I watched as Bertie struggled whilst walking towards me as I sat on the wooden rocking chair, she passed me a brown package with a red ribbon attached to it.

I opened the present in anticipation and looked on in awe as I opened the present, it was a photo album featuring pictures throughout my childhood. The pictures included a photo of us at a beach as young children, a picture of both us dancing in the crop field, and a family photo taken outside of my family home on my first day of high school.

"Where did you find these?" I asked.

"It was the night I escaped the asylum, one of the girls in my Dormitory Gena helped me climb over the fence, she housed me to stand on her shoulders, and with all my strength I pulled up myself over the fence and came crashing down to the ground, grazing my knees, causing my skin to tear, as the blood seeped through. I wrapped my cardigan around my leg and I ran. That night I ran with all my might, and when I reached home, I climbed through the window, grabbed the photo album and spent the night in the barn, before making my way to the ferry, the photos are the only memories we have, I knew Mum and Dad had given up on me." Bertie cried.

"Do you ever think we will see them again?" I asked.

"They chose to abandon us and sent us to that awful place. Maria, you must promise me that you never go back to them, you need to find your own path, and be strong," Bertie ushered.
"I will," I promised.

Bertie seemed to have so much energy that evening, she seemed so happy and so strong. We sat at the dining table and Bertie had a mash dinner whilst I had lasagna. It was the perfect evening. We sat on the couch, talking about our memories as a child, our adventures on the beach, our holidays as a family, and all the party's we had with our family in the barn. We refused to talk about the asylum, and Bertie's illness distracted me from the enduring trauma I was facing. I was so excited for Christmas day, I knew it would be special and a day I would never forget.

I awoke on Christmas day at 7 am, as I peered out of my bedroom window I looked on as the snow lay still, and that when I saw a beautiful deer standing by the tree, looking at me with its bright brown eyes, looking at me startled. I opened the window and watched as the deer ran off into the distance. It felt so wonderful being in the countryside, seeing nature up close, we felt like we were in our own world, hidden away from the outside world.

As I walked into Bertie's room that morning, she looked so pale and weak, her breathing became heavy and she had attached her oxygen mask to her face. I gently sat down on her bed and reached for her hand. "I think it's nearly time," she managed, looking at me with fear as her hand began to tremble. I felt like breaking down in tears, I wanted more time with her, time moved by so quickly in the cottage, there were so many things I wanted to ask her, so much I wanted to say. I decided to lay next to Bertie on the bed. "Is there anything I can do for you?" I asked.

It was then that Bertie waved her weakened arm in the air and pointed at the radio. I turned on the radio, and our song came on 'white Christmas' by Bing Crosby. I was fighting the tears so hard, and then watched as

Bertie passed the locket, I gave her into my hand. That hour we listened to the classic Christmas songs until I felt her hand grip loosen, she slipped away so peacefully. I kissed Bertie on the forehead as tears fell from my cheek onto hers. As I left the room to call the ambulance, I took a deep breath, I had to be strong, I had to fight and carry on but now on my own.

Weeks later I enrolled in the nursing wish after following Bertie's guidance, and moved into the halls of residence, leaving the cottage behind. I collected Bertie's clothes and placed them into boxes and was left with five hundred pounds to help fund my daily living expenses.

I focused all my energies into my nursing course, it helped me to take my mind away from being alone, and every day I fought against my image as the fallen Magdalene girl.

CHAPTER 18: REUNITED

57 years later my life has changed so drastically but my past has haunted me, and my life in the Magdalene asylum has affected my relationships, career path, and day to day interactions.

I look at myself each day, I'm seventy-five, with long grey curly hair,

The wrinkled face, and scars on my back from the harrowing punishment from the nun's in the asylum. I can still see my eighteen-year-old self-running out of the asylum, eighteen years of age, so scared and unsure about the future but desperate to break free from the crutches of the nun's. For 57 years I carried the weight of the events that occurred in the asylum, and the psychological trauma burdened me.

I successfully trained as a nurse and finished my course at the age of twenty-one. I realized I could no longer live in Ireland, and with no family link I had no emotional detachment to stay and I needed to leave to completely avoid the trauma. After my training, I moved to London and gained a role as a nurse in the accident and emergency department for forty years and retired at the age of sixty-three.
I was never able to have a successful relationship and I never married or had children. I was fearful of commitment, fearful of someone else having control in my life, and I fought so hard for my independence.

I had tried so hard to seek help for the trauma I endured, getting counseling support, attending support groups, and taking medication. Writing this book proved to be the most therapeutic and beneficial experience of me, and has helped me come to terms with my experience.

I struggled to keep in touch with Rose, she was always so eccentric and was constantly moving around. The last time I heard from Rose she had become a lawyer and married a successful banker and gave birth to a little girl. I remember seeing her standing outside of Harrods in London, dressed in her striped business suit, her curly red hair glistened in the sun, for once in her life she looked happy.

A few years later I spoke to her husband Derek who expressed that Rose had become an alcoholic and would often fly into rages after a long day of work. Derek explained that he woke up on a Sunday morning and she had packed all her belongings, and no one heard from her again. It was as if she had disappeared.

I tried desperately to track Jane down and was hoping to offer her support. I later discovered later that she had never managed to escape the asylum, and worked there until her death at the age of forty.

For over thirty years I worked as a dedicated nurse, I thrived on helping others and spent many hours training nursing students.
In 1992 shortly after my 50th birthday, I decided to travel to Ireland to finally confront my parents and had planned to go to a support group for the survivors of the Magdalene asylums in Belfast. After taking the long coach journey from the ferry station, I arrived at Enniskillen early on a Saturday morning. I walked up the long-cobbled road and passed the cornfields, and our cottage looked exactly as I remembered it. The treehouse was still in the garden, the white picket fence surrounded the entrance, and the beautiful oak tree stood in the entrance with Bertie's initials carved into the tree.
As I slowly walked up to the house, I peered through the dining room window, sitting on the leather couch was a young couple with their young daughter who held a red rag doll in her hand. Suddenly I heard an automobile pull up at the entrance and the horn beeped. "Can I help you?" asked the lady as she pulled down the window. The lady wore a

bright blue dress and her curly hair was wrapped in a neat bun, her face was wrinkled and tanned, and she bore a scar on her forehead. I recondited the lady as Mrs. Carter, my previous elementary school teacher.

"Mrs. Carter I can't believe it's you! You were my teacher back in

elementary school. I used to live in this house, I'm Maria Sweeney,"

"Maria Sweeney, my goodness I remember you, you were in the
asylum your parents sent you there, how is your sister Bertie?"

"She passed away, over fifty years ago," I added.

"Well do you want me to give you a lift into town?" she asked.

I then hopped into her car awkwardly, nervous at having contact
with my old teacher still feeling judged and persecuted. "Mrs.
Carter You must know what happened to my parents, where did
they move to?" I asked.

"Oh Maria, I'm sorry to tell you that your father passed away over
ten years from a stroke, and your mother resides in the Sisters of
Mercy care home, not far from here."
"Would you take me there?" I asked
"Of course, I will," she added.
I felt so scared and frightened, as I walked up to the American
style care home which was painted white with gold plated gates
and surrounded by apple trees and a ten-acre garden. As I entered
the care home I stood by the common room, whilst the receptionist made an inquiry to find my mother. It was then that I saw
her gazing at me sitting by the window of the common room, in a
red dressing gown and a summer hat. It was sister Rita. I was petrified, her evil green eyes bore into mine, as she gave me the cold
vacant stare. In a desperate panic I ran out of the asylum, falling
to the ground in desperation, I felt as if I had seen the monster's
face, I had tried to avoid for many years. I decided against seeing
my mother, I realized two much time had passed and that I could
never forgive her.

For over fifty years I had not seen my parents and had not been part of a family. In 2019 over fifty-seven years after Bertie had passed away, I received a visitor to my house, a visit that would change my life forever. A man stood at the door with three women. He stood wearing a long brown overcoat, his face was tanned, his hair was sandy brown, and he wore blue-rimmed glasses. Standing next to him was his wife who stood in a red velvet jacket with a grey oval hat. Whilst his identical twins with wild curly brown hair and dressed in matching green jackets stood next to him. I watched as the man took a picture out of his pocket, it was a black and white photo of Bertie from when she was sixteen.

"Are you Maria Sweeney? This is a picture of my mother Bertie, I was told that you live here, can I speak to you?" he asked.

"I was petrified I had always thought about Bertie's son and what happened to him, and now here he was at the age of sixty with his own family. I made everyone a cup of tea and sat close to Brian, he resembled Bertie with his brilliant blue eyes and had freckles on his face.

"How did you find me?"

"I'm a history professor at Oxford University and I managed to track you down through my local library family heritage service."

"I can't believe it, I'm so happy to see you, what happened to you, I believe you were adopted?"

"I was adopted at ten years of age before that I spent time at St Augusta's children's home."

"St Augusta's home? That was only down the road from St Mary's asylum, we were living so close to you."

"I was adopted by a young couple both GP practitioners, they gave me a great life, and after I attended Oxford University, I met my wife Rebecca, and she gave birth to our twin daughters, Lucy and Hannah. I have wanted to find you for years, I know about all the trauma you and my mother experienced and I don't blame you. I want to find out about you and Bertie," he cried, he held onto my hands, trembling before embracing me.

I started to burst out crying, I was in shock, I had felt so alone for so many years. I felt like I was going to become an abandoned old lady, but Brian was the missing piece I needed in my life. "I'm so happy to see you, I'm so glad you've found me, for over fifty years I have been without my family, and now you're here, my very own nephew!"

"You are part of our family now Maria, we can't wait to get to know you," Brian smiled.

For the first time in fifty years I had a family connection again, and would not have to live my life in loneliness

CHAPTER 19: HISTORY OF THE ASYLUMS

The Magdalene laundries were run by the Roman catholic orders between the 18th to the 20th centuries. Over 30,000 women were sent to the asylums in Ireland. In 1993 a mass grave which held 155 corpses was brought to the province and reinforced to the public that suspicious activity was taking place in the asylums. In 2014 the remains of at least 796 babies were discovered in a septic tank in a home called 'the bon secours mother and baby home in Tuam.' Following the discovery of the mass graves, many women came forward to speak of their experiences of the psychological and sexual abuse they endured in the asylums. Many women came forward in the documentary sex in a cold climate in 1997. The Magdalene sisters which was released in 2002, and displayed the criminal practices that occurred in the asylums, whilst also showing the long-term effect of the abuse. The discovery of the mass graves encouraged women to testify about the institutions, and many women believed that the treatment they endured in the asylums violated their human rights. The girls were deprived of nutritious food, vital medications, and were discouraged and prohibited from having any

contact with the outside world. The last known Magdalene laundry which housed 40 women was closed in 1996, the Gloucester Street Laundry.

Many of the women who were sent to the asylum were 'fallen women' including women perceived to have been involved in sexual activity or women that had children out of wedlock. Women who had children out of wedlock were seen as outcasts in society, and as there was no welfare support, women felt there was no choice but to enter the Magdalene asylums. If women were pretty or promiscuous in their behaviour, they would also be candidates for the asylum. It has been discovered that throughout the 19th century different types of women were sent to the asylum, including women who had special needs, women who were raped, and teenage mothers. Women and girls were also sent to the Magdalene laundries after release from prison, instead of being sent to reformatory schools. As many families would disown the married mother following the arrival of the baby. The asylums worked to form a moral reform and made very little impact on a social reform. As the church had a policy of secrecy many of the actions and the register of the number of women in the asylums were never given.

Many of the girls sent to the asylums described the laundry work as painful, many of the girls were forced by the nuns to cut their hair and to change their names. The hours of the laundry were usually from eight in the morning to six in the evening. The state was failing the women in the asylums as they had a duty of care to prevent exploitation and to make the workplace a safe environment for women.

Many of the women felt like they were imprisoned in the laundries as they were locked in and the walls were built high to prevent escape. Living in the asylums proved a very lonely experience for women in the asylum as they were forbidden to talk to others, and friendships and relationships were discouraged. Although the laundries were run for profit the women received no money. The laundry the women washed came from a range of institutions such as public schools and prisons.

It is estimated that over 300,00 women passed through the Magdalene laundries in total.

Many women had to work long hours, often unpaid, with no medical support and little education provision. Many women were told that they could not be paid as they were repenting for their sins. In the 18th century, women were often sent to the Magdalene laundries for short

periods, which was a rehabilitation programme, supported by

the catholic church. The length of stay in the asylums was extended in the 19th century.

Many of the girls that were sent to the asylum spent most of their time at work and had to work around a regime of prayer and laundry work. The majority of asylums were run by nuns. The nuns were having a unique position as they had power over women and young children in society. The government gave contracts to the laundries, without being aware of the treatment and regulation of workers in the asylums.

Many women who were sent to the asylums believe that they were deprived of opportunities in life. They missed out on an adequate education in the asylum and were forced to work in unhealthy and sometimes dangerous conditions. Women were punished for refusing to participate in work, or for refusing to abide by the rules. The punishments included being hit by a cane, and the shaving of hair. Many women reported that they felt lost on leaving the asylum, with no work or no money readily available. Many women fled abroad, as they were never accepted by their families. Women also expressed that the asylums

prevented them from making meaningful relationships in the future. The asylums were only regulated for machinery and factory premises only.

On 19th February 2013, Enda Kenny issued a state apology explaining that the asylums were the shame of the nation. Religious institutions refused to pay compensation to the survivors even after the widely publicized McAleese report in 2013.

In the summer of 2008 in the summer of studying for my history degree, I traveled to Ireland, and I met Maria at a conference in Belfast which discussed the Magdalene asylums. In this meeting, Maria stated she was interested in telling her story. Ten years later we wrote this book together. It was through Maria's story that I learned about the devastating slavery women endured, working in the laundry all day, persecuted by the nun's, and losing their rights to freedom. In meeting with Maria, I learned the true meaning of being a survivor, and found her story and road to freedom inspirational and a true testament to her fighting spirit.

Thank you for reading my book. If you enjoyed it please leave a review.
For updates follow me @markrog90

Printed in Great Britain
by Amazon